EDWIN ARLINGTON ROBINSON

Stages in a New England Poet's Search

David H. Burton

Volume 1
Studies in New England Thought and Literature

The Edwin Mellen Press
Lewiston/Queenston

Library of Congress Cataloging-in-Publication Data

Burton, David Henry, 1925-
    Edwin Arlington Robinson.

    (Studies in New England thought and literature ; v. 1)
    Bibliography: p.
    Includes index.
    1. Robinson, Edwin Arlington, 1869-1935. 2. Poets,
American--19th century--Biography. 3. Poets, American--
20th century--Biography. 4. New England--Intellectual
life. I. Title. II. Series.
PS2719.R526Z59 1986   811'.52 [B]   86-33144
ISBN 0-88946-557-6 (alk. paper)

This is volume 1 in the continuing series
Studies in New England Thought and Literature
Volume 1 ISBN 0-88946-557-6
NETL Series ISBN 0-88946-575-4

The Edwin Mellen Press   The Edwin Mellen Press
P. O. Box 450   P. O. Box 67
Lewiston, New York   Queenston, Ontario
U.S.A. 14092   CANADA L0S 1L0

Printed in the United States of America

TABLE OF CONTENTS

ACKNOWLEDGMENTS

I want to express my thanks to a number of individuals for encouragement and help given in a variety of ways, including Richard Cary, Joseph T. Durkin, S.J., and John P. Mullen. Stephanie Auer graciously undertook typing the manuscript. The editors of *Pacific Philosophical Quarterly* (formerly *The Personalist*), *Thought,* and the *Colby Library Quarterly* kindly granted permission to restate and amplify views originally offered in the pages of their journals.

FOREWORD

A number of books have been written about Edwin
Arlington Robinson and various aspects of his work.
Biographies, assessments of his literary background, and
his philosophical posture -- analyses quite apart from
the piecemeal criticism of his poetry as it was
published -- vie for the attention of those who want to
know something of the author of "Richard Cory," "Miniver
Cheevy," and "Bewick Finzer." A summation of the major
works written about Robinson may help to position the
present study and at the same time suggest reasons for
the particular emphases to be given to his art in the
pages which follow.

Mark Van Doren in <u>Edwin Arlington Robinson</u> (1927)
noted that Robinson saw "life in that profound perspective which permits of it being observed from twin angles
at once ..., realistically and at the same time, ideal-
istically." The tensions present in Robinson's poetry
were the result of this quality of vision. Another
early critic, Lloyd Morris, in <u>The Poetry of Edwin
Arlington Robinson</u> (1923) spoke of "the intensity of his
art and its influence on others." Morris went on to
observe that "in his art he had the disposition to find
in the common experiences of American life the subject
matter of poetry along with a desire to express himself
directly and naturally." The Frenchman, Charles Cestre,
in <u>Edwin Arlington Robinson</u> (1930) commented on
Robinson's seriousness of purpose. Hermann Hagedorn's
<u>Edwin Arlington Robinson</u> (1938) was a biography done by
an old fashioned story teller who had known Robinson

well and one who greatly admired his poetry. Hagedorn acquainted us with the everyday details of the poet's life which Rollo Brown, who lived in proximity to Robinson at the MacDowell Colony, reenforced and enriched in his account, Next Door To A Poet (1937).

Yvor Winters in Edwin Arlington Robinson (1946) and Emery Neff in Edwin Arlington Robinson (1948) were the first to provide in-depth scholarly appraisals. Both noted the intellectual elements in his poetry and wrote about his troubled spirit. Neff in particular under-scored the struggles which were part of his personal life and which influenced his outlook. Meanwhile Estelle Kaplan's Philosophy in the Poetry of Edwin Arlington Robinson (1940) treated the philosophical idealism in Robinson's art; this constituted an important contribution in search of the total Robinson, marred to a degree by the exclusiveness of her claims. A more balanced and a more useful analysis was to be found in Ellsworth Barnard's Edwin Arlington Robinson A Critical Study (1952). This book had two concluding chapters,"Verities" and "Values", in which it was made clear that the poet totally rejected a mechanistic explanation of man in the universe. Barnard also stressed that Robinson's optimism stemmed from being an American.

New ground was broken by Edwin S. Fussell in Edwin Arlington Robinson The Literary Background of a Tradit-ional Poet (1952). Clearly there was more to Robinson's intellectual profile than philosophical idealism. Traditional ways of thinking loomed larger in fact, even though it might be described as a pragmatic traditional-ism. This was the theme taken up by W.R. Robinson in

Edwin Arlington Robinson A Poetry of The Act (1967). In
other words Robinson was prepared to allow old elements
of tradition to be sloughed off if no longer useful as
new elements were accreted according to the prescriptions of a new age. _A Poetry of The Act_ understandably
identified the poet closely with his America and his
fellow Americans.

The 1960's also witnessed the appearance of several
additional interpretations. Chard Powers Smith's _Where
The Light Falls: A Portrait of Edwin Arlington Robinson_
(1965) was a good example of psychobiography, generously
sprinkled with informed guesses about the subject and
his art. Smith claimed that Robinson was "preeminent
among those intellectuals and artists who longed to
discover a meaning to life to replace or revise the
Judaeo-Christian one," a claim which is especially
pertinent to the present study. For Hoyt C. Franchere
in _Edwin Arlington Robinson_ (1968) the poet was most
intent on discovering order in a disordered world yet he
was unable to develop a coherent philosophy which might
have enabled him to do so. Louis O. Coxe's _Edwin
Arlington Robinson The Life of Poetry_ (1969) represented
him as a modernist, which Robinson certainly was, as
well as a traditionalist as much at home in the American
small town as in the metropolis.

One of the purposes of this study is to give
renewed attention to Robinson's response to and reaction
against the historical events, personalities and tendencies in America from the Gilded Age -- he was born in
1869 -- to the New Deal -- he died in 1935. This
amounts to something different from and something more
than an affinity for his country and his countrymen. In

"Annandale Again" Robinson mused:

> "God has been very good to him
> Whose end is not an askingwhy."[1]

In this sense God indeed had not been good to the poet,
whose basic response to the stimulus of life was nearly
always: why? His answer to why? provided perceptive
observations about America and the American experience.
This search often caused him to look at events which,
hardly cosmic, were distinctively American: John Brown
in history or the Prohibition Amendment, for example.
Sometimes his poetry registered dissent, other times it
paralleled developments, and on occasion it anticipated
things to come. Whatever the case Robinson was fully
aware of the flow of change and alive to the imposition
this placed on him as an artist. This explains, in part
at least, the dilemmas discoverable in his art.[2]

The dilemma of the artist in America is the dilemma
of America itself. The Puritans were the first to
experience the contending forces of the spirit and the
frontier, between things as they ought to be and things
as they are. The Quakers,in contrast, made the appropriate compromises: coming to the New World to do good,
they did well. By the eighteenth century materialism
was well advanced. The most celebrated American of the
century was Benjamin Franklin, a worldly philosopher and
the epitome of a materialist ethic. To be sure,
Franklin made worldly success morally attractive,
preachinga kind of Aristotelian middle ground of moderation in pleasure taken and virtue practiced. With the
next century, however, the compromise between spirit and
matter had broken down and serious questions were being

asked by Emerson, Whitman, Thoreau and Herman Melville in the vein of: "whither America?" National purpose and policy, national character and values, America's high destiny were all concerns of these men as their art spoke of the conflicts of their day. The problems giving rise to their dilemmas were oftentimes momentous: transcendentalism or religious orthodoxy, abolition or slavery, union or secession. Edwin Arlington Robinson was heir to all this and revealed much of the American experience of dilemma in his poetic impulse. His times supplied elements peculiar to his own dilemmas, but the dilemma remained for him what it had been from the beginnings of America: a contention between the spirit and the letter, between "ought" and "is", between art and reality as it animates the artist in his work.[3] From Robinson's singular trials as an artist it may be reckoned that artists are closer to the ideas and forces which shape their times than their art may at first convey, that artists too are part of the one woven strip, the great span of life. Edwin Arlington surely was, notice of which is one purpose of this study.

Central to his dilemma was a struggle between good and evil which Robinson portrayed in the lives of people and in the societies of which they were members. This interplay of opposed moral values is not confined to American metaphors though it is nearly always inspired by American experiences. Robinson felt himself free to draw on the full range of Western Civilization, acknowledging barriers of neither time nor space. The setting could be Biblical or contemporary, the character Lancelot or Lincoln but the core of his concern was to identify the contest between good and evil, as these terms were commonly understood by Western man. The variety of situations used is such as to reenforce the image ofRobinson as an artist of sustained moral purpose. Indeed, when a poem is encountered which lacks a moral flavor it is tempting to view it as not authentically Robinson; his playful moments were not numerous. This is not to suggest that Robinson's poetic expression was typically patently spiritual. More often he dealt with the moral problems of everyday people in a sure but oblique way; he was no preacher, however earnest his intention. For him the human race was unified by a common struggle between right and wrong and in his poetry the right did not always prevail. The courage to come to such conclusions was derived to no small degree from the strength he gained in overcoming his own personal weakness which at times threatened to undo him. Instead of falling by the wayside Robinson went on to write great poetry which itself so often delineated the contest between moral and carnal man. In summary Edwin Arlington Robinson saw in his America an object lesson of what ought to be and what was, a drama being acted out in the history of his own country and at which he had a privileged seat.

EDWIN ARLINGTON ROBINSON

ROBINSON

Stages in a New England Poet's Search

I

ROBINSON AND HIS AMERICA

The years marking the life of the poet, Edwin Arlington Robinson, 1869-1935, span the American experience from the Gilded Age to the New Deal.[1] These were years replete with material growth on an almost unprecedented scale, yet punctuated by notable failures in both the material and the moral orders. The wealth of America must be set against social and economic exploitation and cyclical depressions; the world leadership which it prepared to assume was frustrated by a rejection of the Versailles Treaty and with it membership in the League of Nations. America gave the appearance of a man-child, of full stature in might and power, yet uncertain of its domestic priorities and world responsibilities. If not quite the best of times and the worst of times, the era was nonetheless inhospitable to the artist in many ways. Simultaneously, the fast changing conditions challenged the poet, and any number of other observers as well, to provide criticism and understanding. At least that was the way Edwin Arlington Robinson reacted to his times, striving to appreciate and to evaluate the most significant and often most troublesome aspects of a modern America.[2]

Robinson underwent a long struggle before he gained notice as a poet. He was forty years of age when he emerged from the shadows to become a three-time Pulitzer Prize winner and a widely read poet into the bargain.

<u>Tristram</u>, published in 1927, had sales of over twenty-fivethousand copies in three months' time. Along the way to success Robinson was disturbed and even repelled by features of American civilization. He loathed the crass materialism of the business man and his world and came to doubt and distrust the democratic cant of majority rule.[3] Although his feelings in such matters went very deep Robinson, who was "old Yankee" to the core, never thought of taking refuge in a literary exile.[4] Sympathetic with many of the misgivings of the Lost Generation, for example, he could not be counted as one of its members, even by way of courtesy. This was not for example, he could not be simply a matter of age or lack of direct contact with the Great War. His temperament was one of tolerance and patience however intense his feelings, his message one of awareness, not repudiation. Robinson's one trip abroad, to England, he cut short largely because he missed his own country. An "inner voice" told him that he belonged at the MacDowell Colony for Artists that summer of 1923.[5] The result is that E.A. Robinson, like Theodore Dreiser who also spurned exile, remained preeminently American. New World hopes persisted as muted elements in his poetry. Traces of his national inheritance in faint but discernible patterns, they were suggestive of the distance between dream and reality common to the artistic temper.

By remaining at home the poet kept close to the swirling intellectual currents which were rushing America farther and farther away from its past. Often buffeted by these currents, sometimes submerged by the competing demands which tradition and science made upon him, Robinson almost went under before his reputation as a poet was established. Adversity and failures seemed the necessary prelude to achievement. In a sense his career was as self-made as that of any captain of industry. Success did not dim his critical instinct and throughout his life he continued to cast a skeptical eye on war and democracy, on revolution and repression, and on the meaning of man in a modern scientific and technological society. Immersed in America, Robinson was made acutely aware of the dilemma of the artist: to portray the sometimes disturbing realities of lives without despairing of the value of life, to write of the flawed American experience without disdaining the American dream. The raw materials for this poetic exercise lay to hand. Ward McAllister's Four Hundred stood alongside O. Henry's Four Million. The "public be damned" voice of the tycoon competed impressively with the Populist and Progressive demands for reform. The soil of America might prove too thin to nourish the critic of its ways, or, worse than that, America might dismiss such strictures as irrelevant. Robinson was not unlike the character of Lancelot in one of his poems, torn between an adherence to tradition and the appeals of science: "a moth between a window and a star, not wholly lured by one or led by the other."[6] As with artists of every time he had to set his own course, however alien the landscape, and like every explorer of new worlds had no assurance that God would provide. At times, in fact, Robinson was not sure there was a God, so far had America taken him from his ancestral beliefs. Intimations that the age of faith was fast receding were plentiful in the Gilded Age. The signs were there for all to read and Robinson intently scanned them for meaning.[7]

In The Gilded Age success was increasingly judged according to material standards. The heroes of the moment were so many real life Horatio Algers, young men who had bent opportunity into success in the commercial, industrial, and financial spheres. And for every acclaimed success story were thousands of lives modeled on the struggle to excel in the market place but destined for a more modest return on investment. The business of America, it was already clear, was business. No small part of the personal difficulties of Robinson in such a milieu was that he thought this pursuit of dollars was expected of him, a prospect so withering as to cause him to revolt against it. "Dollars are convenient things to have," he wrote his close friend, Harry deForest Smith, in 1900, "but this diabolical dirty race that men are running after them disgusts me."[8] Instead Robinson chose to devote himself, whatever the cost, to the writing of poetry. As he once summed it up, the writing of poetry was "the only thing I was any good at ... there was nothing else I could do, and I had to justify my existence."[9] Such a statement was a tribute not only to what a fellow New Englander of generations past, "Honest John" Adams, once termed "the passion for distinction"; it was also an arresting reminder that every New England conscience, including those of poets, required justification. Edwin Arlington Robinson, as his work was to demonstrate, could escape neither himself nor his Yankee heritage. The tensions discoverable in his poetry were symptomatic of a personal ambivalence which he, in turn, would discover reflected in the America of his day.

Gardiner, Maine, where E.A. Robinson grew up was

typical of New England and the nation in a number of ways and the Robinson family, with its bourgeois values, was hardly remarkable. The industrial revolution came to full flower in the United States after 1865. The year Robinson was born, 1869, saw the incorporation of Standard Oil Company by John D. Rockefeller and his associates, the first million dollar corporation, aside from railroads, in American history. The entire country seemed caught up in the quest for wealth. Agrarian ideals associated with the eras of Jefferson and Jackson no longer held sway, the Senate of the United States had ceased to be a forum for statesmen, and the high resolves of the Civil War were swept aside by the tides of Northern victory. Soon Andrew Carnegie would proclaim a "gospel of wealth," thereby setting the tone and establishing the rationale for the age of capitalistic enterprise. A new generation was being nourished on the belief that the remaining frontiers to occupy were the market place, the factory, the counting house. Immigrants mixed with native sons and daughters, both groups sharing the creed of material advancement. The newcomers readily learned what the old stock had had bred into it, namely, the promise of America was significantly materialistic. In the past this had been leavened with thoughts of liberty, self-government, and great moral movements like Independence and the Union. Now there appeared to be no counter-balancing considerations to dilute the wine of riches and maintain a decent sobriety. Such were the more obvious signs of the times, signs profoundly disturbing to the young Robinson growing up in Gardiner, Maine.

Like numerous other towns Gardiner marched to the new economic drumbeat. If its future was less promising in the overall than many better located places farther south or west, this was not how the town leaders of Gardiner sized up the situation. Among the town fathers was Edward Robinson, the poet's father. As a young enterpreneur he had speculated in standing timber and had reaped handsome profits. Later on he was a store owner, postmaster, money lender, selectman, and legislator. By the time E.A. Robinson was born he had amassed a fortune of some eighty thousand dollars. His mortgages yielded ten to fourteen percent. In a word, Edward Robinson was a man of property. Property for him was a source of pride and power, the reward of a job well done, the indispensable attribute.

What the senior Robinson had become he not unnaturally wanted for his heirs as well. The prospects for the next generation of Gardiner men were promising. There were paper, lumber, and textile mills in or near town while the Kennebec River was both a source of water power and a useful artery for inland commerce. But above all Gardiner and the surrounding area produced vast quantities of ice, ice from the brutal northern winters quarried by Gardiner hands, sold by Gardiner merchants,helping to fill Gardiner's coffers. In all these activities the elder Robinson had an important role. His share of local bank issues alone made him powerful and respected in the community. For him the work ethic had been sufficient to the need, while the expanding economy had done the rest. Not surprisingly, his household was one in which business talk and a business outlook and business values predominated. It might be an unlikely setting for nurturing a poet, or it might prove a rich if perverse kind of encouragement.

Win, as Robinson was called in his boyhood, was the youngest of three sons born to Edward and Mary Palmer Robinson. Through his mother he was a distant relative of Anne Bradstreet, the "Tenth Muse": a New England legend and the only ancestral hint that any of the Robinson clan might possess an artistic streak. This connection with Mistress Bradstreet meant that Robinson was indirectly related to Richard Henry Dana, Wendell Phillips, and Oliver Wendell Holmes, father and son -- all very much part of the New England intellectual and literary tradition -- since he was directly descended from Mercy Dudley, the sister of Anne Dudley Bradstreet.[10] The total of E.A. Robinson's blood was New England, his father's folks having been long settled in Maine. By virtue of this inheritance he shared in the Puritan sense of purpose and of obligation, which expressed itself in "justifying my existence."

Robinson has been described as "an unplanned and an unexpected child."[11] He was in any event different from his two older brothers. Horace Dean, the first son, was twelve years senior to Win. To him Dean was a true hero, going off to college, studying medicine, practicing as a physician. But tragedy struck. Dean became afflicted with acute neuralgia, due in all likelihood to overexposure to the harsh winters of costal Maine. He became addicted to the use of morphine to relieve his pain and quit the practice of medicine some ten years before his death. In the interlude Dean stayed at home, worked occasionally in the Gardiner ice houses, and alternated between pain and the release induced by morphine as the drug slowly destroyed him. He died in 1899.

The bright promise of Dean's career thus sadly tarnished must have had a depressing effect on a younger, worshipful brother. But the total of Robinson's poetry reveals that Dean was also a source of inspiration. In The Pilot, The Dark House, and Captain Craig, the latter one of Robinson's best known poems, the specter of Dean is fully evident. Furthermore, Robinson's fatalistic quality, so often remarked on by critics, is traceable in part at least to Dean's failures. Dean Robinson's story and his place in the storehouse of the poet's mind are better understood in realizing that he had preferred to take up medical research and became a practicing doctor largely at his father's insistence. There was something more tangible (and probably more conventional) in healing the sick than in studying the nature of disease. Edward Robinson was ever the practical man. Not that Win blamed his father for Dean's plight. But such thoughts may have been behind his ruminations to Harry Smith in 1893 when he wrote that "life is a curious mess after all. Sometimes I sit here by my fire and wonder how it is all coming out .... I do not look pessimistically upon the matter. I am inclined to regard it more in the light of a big joke -- whose joke it is, or whether it is a good one, I can not tell."[12] The legacy of Horace Dean Robinson cast a long and troubling shadow over the life of his young brother.

Win also contrasted sharply with Herman Edward, the middle boy. Herman was handsome, gregarious, and popular, well suited to follow in his father's business ventures. But where the senior Robinson was inclined to caution, Herman was impatient to acquire more wealth.

As high as profits might be in Maine, Herman, having been groomed to take over and expand the family fortune, persuaded his father to liquidate a substantial portion of his eastern assets and invest in the west. Herman was an old fashioned plunger, sinking a large part of the Gardiner Savings and Investment Company money (a firm in which his father was a partner) in property in and around St. Louis. He also bought into zinc and copper mines in Minnesota. The years were 1889 and 1890 and the national economy was roaring along. The urge to expand and grow rich was everywhere evident and virtually unquestioned. But overexpansion of industrial capacity as with over-evaluation of property holdings helped to induce the Panic of 1893. The crash in Wall Street reverberated throughout the entire economy. Increased interdependence of the various economic components which had been growing over the course of previous decades meant that the Panic ushered in a long depression, in the face of which the national government proved helpless and from which the country did not emerge until 1896. American politics was convulsed, social unrest was on the rise, and retrenchment became the order of the day. Congress repealed the Sherman Silver Purchase Act which marked a victory for financial conservatives, President Cleveland appealed unsuccessfully to Wall Street to bail the nation out, and Jacob Coxey led an army of unemployed and disgruntled Americans to Washington to seek relief. Meanwhile a smaller drama was being played out in Gardiner. The Missouri real estate investments and the Minnesota mining shares of the Robinsons were wiped out. The tale is a familiar one in accounts of the family in American society as affluence gave way to want. Herman Robinson had no recourse but to come home to Gardiner, an acknowledged failure and looking something of a fool. Not unlike Dean, he sought to shut out reality with alcohol. Though by this time he was married and the father of children, Herman disintegrated under the impact of financial defeat. One day in 1909, he died, alone in the Boston City Hospital, a semi-derelict. And what of Win Robinson in the midst of this family disaster? His response was more calm and more mature than that of his business brother. He and Mary Robinson worked to hold the family together. Dean had to be provided for, and Herman's wife, Emma, and their children. Mary Robinson was no doubt the pillar of strength but she was able to count on Win for help.[13]

E.A. Robinson grew up over-shadowed by older and more experienced and in the last analysis more tragic brothers. Yet he was a normal lad in almost every respect: fond of play and the out of doors, willing and expected to do his chores about the house, and as prepared as the next for a secret smoke behind the barn or innocent romance with the local girls. If he read more than any of his friends, often indulged his introspective strain, and took special delight in curling up in a great chair before the fire to dream away an hour Win, nonetheless, did not stand out from the crowd. Only as he grew older did certain distinctive traits become more pronounced, particularly an interest in serious literature. And as the years rolled by he often pondered the meaning of the lives of his brothers, struck by the emphasis on conventional success and acquisitiveness and the unhappy outcomes, and warned of the dangers involved. It all seemed so wrongheaded, this obsession with success as judged according to the canons of Gardiner. He recognized from an early date how different a person he was from either Dean or Herman and that he must be true to himself, difficult though that might prove to be. In a letter to the literary editor of the <u>Boston</u> <u>Transcript</u>, written in 1913, Robinson touched on this point while trying to define the purpose of his art. "I suppose part of it," he observed, "might be described as a faint hope of making a few of us understand our fellow creatures a little better, and to realize what small difference there is, after all, between ourselves as we are and ourselves not only as we might have been, but would be, if our physical and temperamental make-up and our environment had not been a little different."14 As for himself, Robinson was possessed of his own demon, neither drugs nor alcohol, but poetry. It was a demon to be exorcised only by writing.

In the total family situation Win Robinson, partially neglected by his father and outweighed in Edward Robinson's view by older brothers, grew closest to his mother.15 Never a "mother's boy," he discovered in Mary Robinson a strong but sensitive person. She cared about him and was able to understand her son's craving to be a literary artist. Like the average young woman of her background and station she had written poetry, all of it quite conventional, and had filled copy books with the poetry of others. It was natural for her to encourage Win's literary interests. Among the books she kept in the small house library were volumes of poetry. Drawing down one such book Win read Poe's "The Raven" and was enthralled. His mother was pleased. Mary Robinson was a quiet woman, shy not timid, with a deep and abiding faith according to the Congregational formula. The nurturing relationship she

achieved with her youngest son fitted perfectly the late
nineteenth-century model of the role of wife and mother
and Mary Robinson was satisfied with the prevailing
scheme of things. She had learned to give without
earning the resentment of those she helped. When
Robinson, at the age of twenty-four, told of being
completely dependent on his mother for every penny he
spent, the food he ate, the shelter he enjoyed, he was
observing the facts and not lamenting his fate or
voicing an uneasiness about his mother's love.

Win Robinson entered high school at the age of
thirteen. He took a "scientific" course largely because
his father saw it as practical and because he was to
receive no encouragement to go on to college. Herman
had not attended a college and his career was promising
in a way that pleased Edward Robinson. Dean, the
educated physician, in contrast was even then experiencing the problems which eventually brought him to
ruin. The lesson was clear and college was not to
figure in Win Robinson's future. He did not flourish in
high school, perhaps because of his prospects. Vergil
caught his fancy, or rather Aeneas, the epic hero.
Chemistry amused him. His high school career was otherwise characterized by inattention and indifference to
study. But apart from formal subjects, young Robinson
discovered his need to write poetry. He had been
reading the poets for a year or more. Poe, Shakespeare,
William Cullen Bryant all offered him serious appeal,
and it was to an imitation of the verse style with which
he was familiar that he first turned. By the age of
fifteen Robinson experienced the deeper yearning to be
his own poet, using his own words, betraying his own
feeling, and calling upon a language which was the

language of the day. From the first he had the sense to want to make poetry accessible, not something esoteric or elitist. He displayed a marked democracy of the spirit in this respect, holding that poetry, or at least his poetry, should be read and enjoyed by average people. But this was to be an inconsistent feature of Robinson's mature work because of its considerable intellectual demands on his readers. For the time being he wrote poetry for his own satisfaction, living the life of the novice-artist secretly. He would show his poetry on occasion to some of his classmates, or his Latin teacher. In his third year of high school, when he took up the First Oration Against Catiline, he developed an interest in English blank verse, translating the whole of Cicero's oration into that poetic form. Mostly Win Robinson rejoiced quietly within himself, happy with his good fortune: poetry, the romance of his life, was born.

Though a business outlook pervaded the Robinson household and Gardiner was drawn into the expansion of the American economy to the extent to which its resources allowed, the poetic instincts of Win Robinson received encouragement from others than Mary Palmer Robinson. Gardiner had its literati as any New England town might, a small but dedicated group of men and women for whom literature, both the reading and in some instances the writing of, figured importantly in their lives. The Poetry Society, as Gardiner's literary circle was called, typified the New England tradition. More than any other section of the country the region nurtured this literary bent, honored it with schools and libraries, relied on it to continue to encourage the Emersons and the Thoreaus of later generations. The

town of Gardiner was more favored than most perhaps
because it helped to shape Edwin Arlington Robinson who
would be famous one day. Yet the purpose of the Poetry
Society was to offer its obscure but serious members an
opportunity to discuss, criticize, and very likely
profit from common reading experiences. If an important
poet was spun off in the bargain, so much the better.

Win Robinson joined the Poetry Society soon after
leaving high school and found it easy to feel at home
with its members. It was an indispensible nursery for
his budding interests and its periodic meetings were
something of an oasis for his spirits. Alanson Tucker
Schumann introduced him to the group. A homeopath who
practiced in town and somewhat déclassé according to
Gardiner standards of respectability, Schumann reminded
those who knew him of the thin line which often
separates true genius from mere eccentricity. But he
was a marvelous companion for a young, aspiring poet
because he too was intoxicated with the writing of
verse. As the author of some two thousand poems he was
technically proficient if not very imaginative. What
was important was his sensitivity. This was the common
bond between the man and the youth. The need of the
artist for solitude was balanced by a need for response
and criticism. Schumann was Robinson's first sounding
board, sufficiently critical to be of help and sufficiently friendly to be genuinely concerned. One day not
long after they met, Schumann took him to meet Caroline
Swan, the closest thing to the mistress of a literary
salon a place like Gardiner was likely to have. Herself
derived from solid New England stock she had been among
the first graduates of Radcliffe. After living in
France she came back to Gardiner to teach school and to

care for an aged mother. Caroline Swan had been one of
Schumann's teachers, she contributed to the Atlantic
Monthly, and was a remarkable woman in her own right.
She greatly admired the French poets, Ronsand and
Verlaine especially, and translated much of their verse
into English. Her interest lay both in technique and
message but for Robinson at this early stage of his
development, technique was everything. He was confident
that in time he would have his own ideas and his own
message. What he needed first was to master form. The
French forms were intricate and demanding. Had he come
to them alone and unaided he would have been at something of a loss. But in the company and guidance of
Schumann and Caroline Swan, and Henry Sewall Webster,
another Gardinerite who was a judge by profession and a
poet by instinct, Robinson began to settle in quietly
and comfortably with the prospect of writing poetry as a
life's work. Furthermore the love of literature evident
in his friends of the Poetry Society fueled his growing
belief that worldly success could be less than satisfying even to those who had attained some measure of it.
The vaguest intimations of Robinson's quandary as an
artist he now experienced. On the one side stood his
father's values: practical, tangible, obtainable; on the
other were the aspirations of the spirit: moral, opaque
and elusive. No final decision had been made but the
drift of his preference for the spiritual world appeared
more pronounced.[16]

Robinson gained a great deal from his small town
upbringing, the small town as the cradle of the great
majority of American success stories in the nineteenth
century, whether in business or the arts. There was for
the poet a hazy innocence in the Gardiner way of life

which tended to enlarge as he looked back upon it year after year, especially his childhood years before the moral tensions had sprung up. In his fondness for his home town he was not alone. When young men went out to the cities to seek their fortunes, or to write poetry, they endowed their home towns with what was perhaps an exaggerated sense of the old fashioned values. They respected those values in theory, even as they admitted they were not easily maintained in the drive for material success. In his poems Robinson sometimes alluded to the lost places of his youth. Perhaps too much scorn has been heaped on Gardiner in an interpretation of Robinson's poetic mind because he eventually disowned much of what it stood for. Nonetheless the conflict between what he chose to remember of the sunny days of his Gardiner childhood and the gloomy nights of his later big city ordeals was part of the dilemma of the artist. In America in general this same antipathy obtained. Small towns and adjacent farms no longer held out the promise of the rewards or the life style which people preferred; the city was the magnet drawing all those seeking opportunity and success. Rural America, village and farm alike, had fallen on hard times.[17] America was in the throes of change, much of it dueto the rise of an industrial economy, but it was change traceable also to the intellectual ferment associated with new scientific theories.

The intellectual history of the American people underwent striking alterations in the years of E.A. Robinson's coming of age. Over the final decades of the nineteenth century the ancient doctrine of supernaturalism, in which a divine Christ was the distinct element in natural events as well as in the affairs of men, was directly challenged by new developments in the biological and natural sciences. The result was a delimitation of the supernatural order so profound as to influence literature and education, philosophy and religion, and the arts in their various expressions. It would be a number of years before this influence would filter down to the masses, but for the alert and curious intelligence of some one like Robinson, who was in increasing intercourse with the world of ideas as represented by Dr. Schumann and Caroline Swan, the impact was almost immediate. Rather typically for example, he became more and more aware of the incompatibility of a literal rendering of Genesis and the scientific assertions about the origin and age of the universe, with results immensely significant for his outlook.

American religion was in a state of flux. Theosophy and Christian Science had already been added to the list of religions which the country seemed capable of spawning in response to fashions no less than to scientific inquiry. Many of these new religions with their element of the mysterious were, paradoxically, as vulnerable to scientific attacks as the established orthodoxies. In any case the school of higher criticism of the Christian Scriptures, if its conclusions were to be honored, cast grave doubt on belief of any sort. Discoveries in the fields of anthropology and comparative religion tended to strip Christianity of its uniqueness. The Bible gradually ceased to be a source of religious faith for many and became instead a literature rich in the understanding of man. In 1892 Charles A. Briggs, a leading Presbyterian clergyman, was acquitted in a heresy trial for asserting that "all a priori definitions of inspiration are not only unscient-

ific, but irreverent, presumptious, lacking in the
humility with which we should approach the divine,
spiritual fact." The vindication of Charles Briggs
represented an important triumph of science among men of
religion. Robinson, in a defiant mood, could write to
Harry Smith that his "vision of Trinity Church in Boston
and a reflection of what it stands for" made him "feel
like breaking chairs and wondering if a time is ever
coming when the human race will acquire anything like a
logical notion of human life ...."[18] The stature of the
churches was diminished in the eyes of many because as
institutions they appeared to be against change and
progress, according to the dispensations of Social
Darwinism.

In the purely scientific realm the challenge to
revealed religion was direct and immediate. Physics was
thought to hold the key to the new astronomy of stellar
structure and its evolution. Such theories as the
Second Law of Thermodynamics with its rule of the
dissipation of the energy of the earth were irreconcil-
able with Christian ethics. The bases of life were
described in chemical terms, while the biological
analogies drawn from Darwin proposed to ordain a new
orthodoxy. For every scientist who was to agree with
Asa Gray's position that Darwinism had done no harm to
Christianity there were a dozen who concluded that
religious faith, as distinguished from ethics, was no
longer relevant. Eventually Robinson's generation and
Robinson himself would be faced with the choice of
reconciling religion and science, or rejecting reconciliation in favor of one position or the other. For
religion the upshot was not promising. To accept
scientific materialism was to condemn human life to the

quaint adventure of the protoplasm. To embrace Christianity as a faith in God, even mildly, was deemed anti-
intellectual. For many reconciliation was the most
promising road to follow. John Fiske in Outline of
Cosmic Philosophy (1874) held that evolution was merely
part of the divine plan. Rev. Henry Ward Beecher in
Evolution and Faith (1885) declared that evolution was
but a "deciphering of God's thought as revealed in the
structure of the world." But for the artistic temper
which tended to reject easy compromise such formulas
were less than satisfying. Throughout his work Robinson
struggled to achieve his own peculiar resolution of this
dominating problem, adding thereby a richness of detail
to his spiritual wanderings.[19]

E.A. Robinson attended Harvard in the early 1890's
and his years there were something of a watershed,
storing ideas and impressions which he was able to draw
upon in the lean days of artistic obscurity. Though he
was ill-prepared for college by reason of his high
school training and had given up hope of going on to
college he did attend lectures at Harvard for two years
after all. It was a piece of misfortune which enabled
him to enjoy the good fortune of Harvard. For a number
of years he had experienced a disorder of the ear. Sent
to Boston for examination by a specialist, it was
discovered that the drum of one ear was broken and the
bones diseased. The doctor thought it not too late to
save Robinson from serious complications if the ear
could be treated promptly and on a regular basis over an
extended period of time. Such treatment could be had
only in Boston. Edward Robinson reluctantly agreed to
Herman's suggestion which would allow Win to enroll at
Harvard in order to occupy his time while receiving the

necessary medical attention. He sat as a special student at Harvard, beginning in September, 1891.

The Harvard of that era had become a reflection of President Eliot's much heralded elective system. It was a system ready-made for Robinson's needs. In as much as he did not matriculate for a degree the overall flexibility of the curriculum enabled him to pick and choose his lectures without being conspicuous. At first Robinson was overly conscious that at twenty-one years of age he was not a typical college freshman. He was content to enroll in elementary courses in English composition and in French, another in nineteenth century prose, as well as one in Shakespeare and a course in Anglo-Saxon, "more for the discipline than anything else." As staggered as any freshman by the initial workload, at month's end he had regained his equilibrium. Thereafter he settled in for two of the happiest years of his life.

Under President Eliot's guidance Harvard had made its way from a "recitation" style of learning popular as late as the 1860's. According to it students were receptacles into which were poured carefully measured amounts of "knowledge" [and against which the likes of Oliver Wendell Holmes, Jr. had revolted]. Now the university's main purpose was to encourage students to think honestly and critically. Other American universities were soon emulating Harvard. The faculty in Robinson's time included Charles Eliot Norton and Josiah Royce, William James, Francis Child, and in the midst of these and other worthies, a young and vibrant George Santayana. The air was electric with great ideas just as the university was graced by great scholars and thinkers. In his first year Robinson's favorite was Lewis Gates lecturing on the nineteenth-century prose writers. He never missed a Gates lecture and while he might take his share of cuts from other courses he remained on balance a serious student. In his own view he got more out of his first year of college than many of his fellows. The second year's work proved more demanding than the first and Robinson worked that much harder. He was especially keen on Norton's Fine Arts 3. Norton was a master teacher, an ideal spokesman for the glories of antiquity and altogether anxious to set them against the distasteful realities of the mauve decade. Norton's course, inadvertently perhaps but nonetheless significantly, touched on the dilemma with which the artist must deal: to value the ideal and to learn to live with the reality without despairing of the ontological fact of both. Norton opened up vistas, and occasionally yawning chasms, for Robinson to think on. Could the enduring values, for example, resist the materialistic tide? Were men destined to abandon art in favor of technology? Was civilization retreating before a scientific barbarism? The watershed was building up reserve. Another great mind which touched Robinson in his second year was that of Josiah Royce. The subject to be studied in Royce's philosophy was "the spirit of modern philosophy." Robinson brought to Royce's thinking his own version of Emersonian Idealism. The "know-thyself" elements which were to be a feature of his mature poetry and which were derived from a mixture of the old Puritan conscience and nineteenth-century Transcendentalism discovered a fresh stimulus in Royce. Of the many aspects of his complex philosophy the one with the built-in appeal to Robinson was Royce's emphasis on Self. Self was both a consciousness of its

conformity with the harmony of the universe and a
component of the larger Self which is the universe.
When a contemporary philosopher was able to supply both
a conscience and a world order through the unifying
device of Self E.A. Robinson was likely to listen, with
one ear at least.[20]

The place of Royce in the development of Robinson's
artistry in so far as it was informed by a philosophical
system should not be judged by whether or not Robinson
became an Idealist. Robinson was unaffectedly
intellectual because he was so much an artist. Through
the work of Royce he was encouraged to allow full range
to the skepticism implied in Idealism rather than to
embrace the dogmatic fatalism implied in scientific
materialism. If at any time this variant of skepticism
led Robinson down the path of agnosticism one should not
be surprised. Any number of his contemporaries held an
agnostic position, sometimes on the basis of reasoned
argument and sometimes on a wave of emotional backlash.
Robinson's agnosticism must be appraised on rational and
irrational grounds just as, at times, his faith appears
to have rested on the same two attitudes. The Puritan
trait in his work indicated that he was talking not only
about material things but also about heaven and hell in
the human soul. Given his inheritance as well as his
personality Robinson probably could not have examined
significantly the problems of lives in his America
except for the stimulus derived from the critical temper
of the modern mind. Royce was one source of that
critical temper. By no means was he an unquestioning
disciple of Royce but the times in which they lived
produced in the poet, as it had in the philosopher, a
need to understand the universe in more than corporeal
terms.21

Royce appealed to Robinson's strongly introspective personality. The ancient Puritan faith which he had inherited had been drastically diluted. Some individuals might cling tenaciously to its orthodoxies but for increasing numbers Emerson had replaced Edwards as the high priest of Puritan beliefs as these had become transliterated into a New England ethic. After the erosion which had come with succeeding generations there still stood at the center of the New England outlook the mighty fact of conscience.[22] Many attempted to rationalize it in terms of the new psychology, or to ignore it in the name of the new science, or delude it in the name of the old concupiscence. Indeed, Robinson was to indulge in all three of these escapes at one time or another, only to come away with the conclusion that the persuasions of conscience were ineluctable.

To a seeker after truth like Robinson Ralph Waldo Emerson had had something to say. He was certainly influenced by Emerson and the whole of the Transcendentalist theses that human beings were best witnessed through the cultivation of each individual's special aptitude. While at Harvard Robinson read Emerson's The Conduct of Life, explaining that Emerson "took him over his knees and walloped him with a big New England shingle for about three-quarters of a New England hour."[23] Perhaps Emerson's influence added up to no more than some gentle persuasions which he worked on numerous other sensitive people who read his Essays and who were convinced by his feeling of man's transcendent worth. But if Emerson's optimism was infectious, Robinson seems to have remained somewhat immune to that

side of the sage's teaching. His own personal and
family experiences were too strong a barrier. Apart
from Emerson Robinson had other influences competing for
his attention and allegiance. He was also reading
Thomas Hardy at this time, for example, and finding in
him a "marvelous mixture of humor and pathos."[24]

The total educational experience which Robinson
enjoyed at Harvard must be judged both in terms of his
professors and his fellow students. Francis Child, for
example, introduced him into the mysteries of Anglo-
Saxon, A.S. Hill added vigor to an existing predilection
for niceties of language and he greatly admired the
learning of George Lyman Kittredge without ever
presuming to emulate it. Still these men came to mean
less to him than his peers, some of whom were to become
friends for life. He encountered Mowry Saben early in
his Harvard days and was greatly taken with him. Saben
may have been a genius, he was indubitably eccentric,
and attractively pagan. Another significant friendship
was struck with George Burnham, then beginning Law
School. Burnham's personal tragedies wedded him at once
to Robinson's compassionate self. The names of others
are less important than the fact that Robinson was one
of a circle, which styled itself "the corncob club" and
which had as its sole reason for existence the free and
open discussion of men and ideas, those encountered at
Harvard and in their range of literature which was ever
widening. Inevitably the talk of the "corn cobbers"
would get round to God. One member, Tryon, was studying
Newman and the Oxford Movement, another Hubbell, was a
Swedenborgian; Saben the pagan added zest to the discus-
sions while Burnham knew enough of Oriental religion to
provide still another dimension. Edwin Arlington

Robinson, however, remained the seeker, an attitude he
retained throughout his life; like his America he was no
longer permitted the easy adherence to ancient faiths.
The work of Freud combining with the higher criticism of
the Bible promoted turmoil when it came to an attempt to
conceptualize God. For the time being Robinson was
content to be a Unitarian. Touched by Emerson, he
admired much in Carlyle. "Carlyle has given me a brush
lately, and I am beginning to see what he was driving at
in his Sartor Resartus," he told Harry Smith about this
time. "If the book is anything it is a denial of the
existence of matter as anything but a manifestation of
thought. Christianity is the same thing and so is
illuminated common sense," he concluded.[25] In short,
Robinson enjoyed the intellectual relativism characteristic of Harvard in the 1890's, using the opportunity to
develop as an eclectic thinker and thus eventually a
protean artist. Part of his fascination as an artist
rests in that consideration. At one time or another,
for example, he was to imagine himself as a Christian, a
Hindu, an agnostic. His art was not confined to any set
formula, just as the larger American mind,of which
Robinson was a small but instructive part, acquired a
variety of shadings. Harvard, in its formal instruction
and informal pursuits, opened windows on the world for
Win Robinson.

Harvard gave no answers for the future poet as to
the meaning of life. It had posed a series of questions
to which he would endeavor to respond over the course of
his poetic output. Meanwhile he returned to Gardiner in
1893, the medical attention given him at the Massachu-
setts General Hospital having worked to arrest the
disease of the ear. Once back home Robinson was face to

face with the problems which had laid a kind of seige to his family. 1893 was the fateful year of the Wall Street Panic. By then his father was dead, Dean was a ghost of his former self, and Herman proved no match to the financial disaster which engulfed him. Win Robinson was quick to help where and how he could, but he refused to throw over his art for the sake of getting a job. It was a clash between the bourgeois morality of Gardiner and his devotion to the writing of poetry. The poems which he had been writing over the years (he had published a few in The Harvard Advocate while a student and some had been rejected when submitted singly to various magazines) Robinson gathered together in book form, The Torrent and the Night Before. He published this slim volume in 1896, at his own expense, 312 copies, dedicated to "any man or woman who would cut the pages." In some ways this was a desperation effort to gain a modicum of recognition, Robinson sending copies to numerous editors and critics. What notices he got were encouraging, but inconclusive, one critic writing "you will do better if you are yet young."26 The next year Robinson's good friend and Harvard classmate, Will Butler, underwrote the cost of a 500-copy edition of a second collection, published under the title, The Children of the Night. In it appeared some of the poet's best known short verse, including "Richard Cory." The Children of the Night, in retrospect at least, signalled the emergence of E.A. Robinson, though it would be years before he achieved a reputation.

The poems collected in The Children of the Night included some valuable clues to Robinson's personal dilemmas as well as those of the poet as an artist. "Calvary," one of the short poems, had a strongly traditional, it might even be fairly said, pietistic, turn to it. "The Master trod along to Calvary;/ We gibed him, as he went, with houndish glee" were lines betraying reverence and quite possibly belief.[27] The poem ended on an ethical note, but one which presupposed the historical Calvary, and what that had connoted to succeeding generations. In another short verse, "The Altar," Robinson tended to think both scientifically and traditionally, describing man as "Bewildered insect plunging for the flame/ That burns, and must burn somehow for the best."[28] But in "Zola", perhaps for the first time in his published work, he touched on the dilemma of the artist. Zola was the seeker of Truth, and for that he was loathed by many. Zola saw "the human heart/ Of God meanwhile, and in His hands was weighed/ Your squeamish and emasculate crusade/ Against the grim dominion of his art."[29] Zola had not permitted disapporval to sway him from the trust. Robinson was saying that the artist must always pay the price.

Meanwhile there was a life to live, despite the gloomy Robinson family situation. His mother had died of "black diphtheria" in 1896 and Dean lived only until 1899. The ties that bound him to Gardiner were snapping one by one. Still his arrival as a published poet, if one too little read, enabled him to make new and worthwhile friends in Gardiner. One of these was Laura Richards, a daughter of Julia Ward Howe, a woman of understanding and compassion; another was John Hays Gardiner, a Harvard faculty member who was to rescue the struggling poet on several occasions. He also enjoyed the company of the Quadruped, a foursome of like-minded young men who met periodically to talk poetry and music. Yet somehow Gardiner was not enough. Robinson had lived briefly in New York in 1897 and found it immensely attractive and ... liberating. In 1899 he spent some six months at No. 5 University Hall on the staff of President Eliot but he had no stomach for academic routine. The passing of Dean Robinson in September of that year was all that was needed to break with home. New York, "the town down the river," was beckoning him, as it was a whole new generation of artists.

E.A. Robinson's departure from New England and his deliberate choice of New York as a place to live and write raises a question regarding his place in the Indian Summer of New England's literary history. Although he would remain a State of Mainer all his days and many of his pieces would identify him with the "bleak and bare" of rock-bound coasts, Robinson saw in New York the chance to survive as an artist, and if not, as a human being. His poetry was cramped by his home-land memories and its realities. He needed fresh air to breathe, he needed to escape from an environment which never failed to produce in him a gnawing anguish about his refusal to seek and find worldly success. No one in New York was likely to pose such questions. At least that highly personal aspect of his artistic quandary could be set aside. In removing himself from Gardiner, or even Boston, Robinson had helped to sustain rather than abandon the literary life of New England. By the close of the nineteenth century America had grown too large and complex to have its literary impulses confined to one area or one city. If William Dean Howells felt impelled to come to Boston in the 1880's because he needed to do so as a budding author, for much the same reason Robinson had to go to New York. The city had grown important in commerce and trade, cosmopolitan in

character and appeal, large in variety and numbers.   In
the process it had produced its own literary bohemia,
Greenwich Village, which had a magnetic appeal for
artists of all sorts and degrees of recognition.   New
York was very much Robinson's kind of place.   The New
England side of his artistry continued alive and persuasive, nonetheless.   Along with many others he helped to
make the transition of literary America from a place to
a state of mind.   The adulterations resulting from this
transition were relatively minor for Robinson personally, a reminder of Robert Frost's remark that "Yankees
are what they always were."

II

THE GREENING OF A POET

E.A. Robinson realized something of the liberation he longed for when he moved to New York City in 1899, in his own phrase, "for six months or a life time."[1] Whether he would be able to win recognition as a poet was another matter. The prospects were not reassuring. Could a feckless poet of thirty-odd years somehow break through the wall of indifference signalled by the tepid reception of his early published verse? Even critics who discovered qualities to praise in The Children of the Night appeared to be looking past Robinson, as though in search of another talent who could be celebrated as the harbinger of a new wave of poets. Without being completely discouraged, Robinson himself was aware of this and helpless to do much about it. For the moment, at least, New York City was enough; the romance of Bohemia seemed very real. To vary the later phrase of Al Smith, Robinson rejoiced in the idea that in New York he had five million neighbors.

The move to New York City was in keeping with a rising consciousness of the place of the city in the fermentation of new literary and artistic forms. The two best novels of William Dean Howells, The Rise of Silas Lapham (1885) and A Hazard of New Fortunes (1895), with their plots unfolding in Boston and New York respectively, showed the way in this regard and portrayed the city in such fashion as to identify the convergence of the creative artist and an urban milieu. Like Henry James, Howells found in the city a place where the drama of conflicting human values was especially affecting. Mark Twain, Stephen Crane, and Willa Cather at one time or another all had represented city life with sympathy, while to Theodore Dreiser, as in Sister Carrie (1900), the city was a temptress, with "cunning wiles." Dreiser saw in the city "large forces which allure with all the soulful expressions possible in the most cultured human. The gleam of a thousand lights is often as effective as the persuasive light in a wooing and fascinating eye," he remarked. In preferring the city Robinson demonstrated the same attitude as George Washington Cable and Walter Hines Page, men who deemed it impossible to live in their native places and who sought the metropolis out of creative necessity. A generation later Thomas Wolfe gave expression to the lure of the cities with their "immense and glorious stations, murmurous with their million destinies and the everlasting sound of time."[2] In his short piece, "Boston," Robinson spoke his own attraction to the city when he wrote:

> My northern pines are good
>   enough for me,
> But there's a town my memory
>   uprears --
> A town that always like a
>   friend appears,
> And always in the sunrise by
>   the sea.
> And over it, somehow, there
>   seems to be

        A downward flash of something
            new and   fierce,
        That strives to clear, but
            never clears
        The dimness of a charmed
        antiquity.[3]

Though it possessed the allure of the city for Robinson
he was not making an unqualified commitment to Boston as
a friend. Throughout much of his poetry Robinson would
remain enthralled by the "dimness of a charmed
antiquity."

The New York to which E.A. Robinson came was a metropolis not unlike other American cities in the problems
which it faced. In the eyes of the Progressive reformers of the period to save the city was to save the
nation itself from impending social and economic
disasters. Political corruption had been a feature of
New York ways at least from the heyday of Boss Tweed and
Tammany Hall. Even a young, aggressive Police Commis-
sioner like Theodore Roosevelt had found it impossible
to overcome the system; he resigned his office in 1895
rather than endure continued frustrations in attempting
to enforce the law. In The Shame of the Cities Lincoln
Steffens gave readers vivid impressions of the extent of
official malfeasance, but while reform movements rose
and fell political corruption was a virtual constant.

The physical health of the inhabitants of the cities
was a further persistent worry because of poor nutri-
tion, squalid living conditions, and plain ignorance.
Threat of fire to human habitation in the tenement
districts as well as in factories must be added to any

list of social problems. Not that some progress under
the law was not made. In New York, for example, on the
urging of Lawrence Veiller a State Commission was
established in 1900 to study tenement life and to
propose corrective measures. Out of the Commission's
investigations came recommendations incorporated in New
York's Tenement Law of 1901 which made provision for
stringent fire precautions, baths for every family, and
similar improvements. Implementation of such laws would
be another matter, but a start had been made. Among the
most important voices raised in the name of the city's
poor was that of Jacob Riis. His book, How The Other
Half Lives (1890), exposed the physical wretchedness and
the moral degradation of the miserable ghettos of the
poor. Lower Manhattan was his special haunt. The area
was a veritable nursery of success and failure, of
criminals and, occasionally, a philosopher. One of the
latter, who was to become a good friend of Edwin
Arlington Robinson many years later, was Morris Raphael
Cohen.[4]

Morris Cohen had been born in Minsk, probably in
the year 1880, the fifth or sixth child of hard-driven
if not oppressed parents. At the age of twelve he left
Russia with his mother and sister, following his father
who earlier had migrated to America. The family settled
in New York City. The rise of Morris Cohen from the
hard times of the Lower East Side by means of school,
college, and university is a variation on the classic
American success story. He took his Ph.D. at Harvard in
1906 and for many years thereafter taught at City
College in New York. Bertrand Russell judged him to be
the most original American philosopher of his generation. The contrast between the background and upbring-

ing of Robinson, the old stock Yankee, and Cohen, the
New World immigrant, was pronounced, but Robinson, like
Cohen, took great delight in befriending all manner of
men and women. In his autobiography, A Dreamer's
Journey (1949), Cohen paid tribute to Robinson's help
which enabled him, he said, to appreciate the peculiar
genius and role of the artist in civilization. As a
young thinker Cohen had held stubbornly to the view that
aestheticism and democratic ideas were inherently
hostile. Rare paintings and fine music, he thought,
added nothing to one's understanding of human nature or
society. A pluralist, he found enough anthropological
evidence to support his position that "talk about
superior taste may mean blindness to its [life's]
natural diversity." As a result of many conversations
with Robinson Cohen related how he changed his judgments. Just as "only a few who are highly trained
understand the meaning of scientific laws," he was led
to conclude that "in the field of art too training may
make clear what is otherwise vague and indistinct."
Robinson had played a vital part in bringing Cohen to
appreciate that "people see and hear what great artists
have taught them to see and hear." This conversion to
aestheticism was to occur very much in the future when
the two men came to know one another at the MacDowell
Colony for Artists in the 1920's; yet Cohen's life is
suggestive of the richness and variety of the city to
which Robinson was attracted and where he was to
establish his reputation.5

The immediate prospects for recognition were nonetheless discouraging. To follow Robinson's path and to
examine his life style during the first half-dozen years
in New York points directly, in Riis's phrase, to "how

the other half lived." It is at the same time an opportunity to recount some of the most telling experiences which the city provided him as he strove to develop his poetic talents. At first Robinson was alone, as a consequence of which perhaps he became a heavy drinker. He was to remember these first years as a time when he "had absolutely nothing but the bottle."[6] There was the real chance that in the end this indulgence would destroy him and his art in much the same fashion that had brought ruin to his brothers. A limited income drawn from the residue of his family's estate grew smaller and smaller and before long it was gone. During the whole of this time, down to 1905, Robinson relied on friends to sustain him. John Hays Gardiner was perhaps his chief source of the odd sums required to keep him from going under completely, but others occasionally supplied money as well. All this was no small tribute to the kind of enduring faith Robinson inspired in people and the hidden promise of his poetry in which a few continued to believe. His dissoluteness dramatized the loneliness of urban existence, removed as he was from family and native place. Roving from one address in the city to another, pursued by "the competent bedbug," eating saloon lunches, living with and off friends, E.A. Robinson drifted across New York like a man torn between search and escape.[7] Somehow he never lost sight of the purpose of his existence: to write poetry. "Captain Craig," one of his major poems, which was a product of these early New York days, made this plain. Altogether this period was the long night of Robinson's artistic soul, a necessary prelude to the work of the mature poet.

It would be an oversimplification if not a distortion to insist that Robinson first encountered the character of Captain Craig in his wanderings about New York. It is certain that there were elements of his brother, Dean, in his delineation of Captain Craig. But there was one particular friend from the city upon whom he modeled much of what he fashioned in the poem. He was Alfred Louis. Louis was a literary vagabond whom Robinson met one day while in the editorial office of The Century Magazine. About sixty years of age he was a kind of hero-failure to whom the poet was instinctively attracted. Born in England and a Jew who converted to Catholicism, Louis had been educated at Cambridge and claimed to know many of the literary giants of the time. He was both absurd and appealing. Robinson dismissed his foibles to concentrate on what he was sure was his wisdom. Alfred Louis was just the sort of individual most likely encountered in the big city, part of the human flotsam common to London, Paris, or New York. Cities were his natural habitat. For that matter the whole story of the travails of the manuscript of "Captain Craig" carried a big city stamp. Having completed the work Robinson sent it off to the Boston firm of Small, Maynard and Company where his Gardiner friend, Laura Richards, had used influence to persuade the editor to consider the submission. But the publisher's reader left the manuscript in what Robinson delicately referred to as a "house of seclusion." There it remained for some months under the care of the madam, to be retrieved by the reader on a subsequent visit. After further delays and the addition of other poems to make up a new collection, entitled Captain Craig, it was published by Houghton Mifflin. Hays Gardiner and Laura Richards had provided the necessary subvention.

What Robinson had done in the title poem of this collection was to provide an intensely sympathetic portrait of an anti-hero. In his development of the character, Craig was a kind of revolutionary figure, in much the same sense that Christ has been interpreted as a revolutionary. To one friend he was quick to explain that Craig was also "something of a scholar, but not `me' as I fancy you have suspected."[8] In keeping with his expressed conviction that "Art is only valuable to me when it reflects humanity,"[9] Captain Craig stood for Robinson's version of humanity in all its flawed nobility.

The poem itself was the story of a spiritual success achieved in spite of, or because of, worldly failure.[10] It was an outstanding example of Robinson's favorite theory: "the success of failure." Craig was a bedraggled ne'er-do-well, a nice compound of wit and wisdom, "of lettered nonchalance," whose life was saved by five or six men of Tilbury Town. They had taken pity on Craig and restored him to health. Their act was a matter of unalloyed charity. In his turn Captain Craig drew upon his ample treasury of wisdom, inate and acquired, to hold forth to them on the meaning of life. In the course of his soliloquies Craig was heard to profess the ideals which seemed very close to Robinson's own humanized faith. Craig's character spoke the high aspiration of mankind. His failures had induced in him no sense of hate or recrimination. Instead he was "without a curse/Without a murmur even."[11] Craig was quietly resigned to his fate. But interest in the poem centered less on Craig and more on the observations he made about life, and for which Robinson had a deep and

abiding respect. Like the poet, Craig was caught up in
the dilemma of the artist because their sensitivities
were kindred. Robinson proposed to evaluate man in a
way reflecting the Western tradition when he wrote:

> "Nothing is there more marvelous than man,"
> Said Sophocles; and he lived long ago.[12]

This nobility had a rational basis and a sane purpose.
The basis was the spiritual nature of man, unique among
worldly creatures, a nature which if thwarted or denied
made man less than man. It was this spirituality "That
makes you craven or invincible/ Diseased or puissant
..."[13] The nobility of men, furthermore, augured much
good. "What power a man has in him to put forth,"
marveled Captain Craig.[14] Men had the opportunity not
only of aiding their fellow human beings in a material
way, but more importantly for Robinson, of helping them
spiritually. Robinson had Craig relate how a soldier by
the kindness of his actions had saved a young man from
suicide. The beauty of the act derived from an inherent
spirituality, so that pondering the event Craig spoke of
the power for good in men which was not an accident of
worldly beings. Robinson had too much tact and sense of
humor to assume the role of preacher in "Captain Craig,"
yet he offered a humanized Christian message of faith
and hope and charity, one of the most moving and lucid
in the full range of his philosophical statements.

Though later recognized as important, "Captain
Craig" and the other poems in the collection did not win
a ready acclaim. Critics objected to the chopped effect
of Robinson's blank verse while finding some passages
"shot through with real poetic fire." He was described

as having a "positive talent" for narrative poetry but the rhymed poems, some critics judged, were marked with obscurity. The collection was far from a failure but equally distant from a success. This is not unexpected. As T.S. Eliot has pointed out, in these years the situation of poetry was stagnant to a degree difficult for any young poet of a later period to imagine. Robinson would have to continue to suffer and to pay for his devotion to art, sufficiently encouraged by whatever the critics had deemed acceptable in his poems and by his own faith as well.

In his personal life, however, Robinson reached a new low in the years immediately after publication of Captain Craig. His habits became increasingly derelict. He remained in touch with a few friends, including Mowry Saben recently returned from Europe with renewed enthusiasm for the prospect of converting the human race to his peculiar formula of humanistic ethics. But such contacts as Robinson had with Saben and others were less frequent and less meaningful. No doubt he brooded over his fate and the strange and troubling circumstances of his life at Gardiner and afterward. He managed to write little poetry in the dark, narrow quarters he occupied on West 23rd Street. Robinson was down and out, one of the city's cast-offs, learning afresh the nature of the bargain he had made to devote his life to poetry, contra mundum.[15]

There was nothing in the bargain which prevented him from taking a job, as distinguished from career employment. Besides, he was destitute and had to make up his mind whether, literally, to live or to die. These circumstances appear the only explanation of his willingness -- a very reluctant willingness -- to take a job as a timekeeper on a New York subway construction project in 1903. Unused to the physical labor, which included spending hours underground in the damp semi-darkness, Robinson was played out by his tasks. He returned to the work day after day largely for the $2 wage he was paid. With only Sundays off, about all he could to was to reassure himself that the experience was worth the grief. And it no doubt was. He liked his fellow workers and they became fond of him. Exposed to mostly immigrants on a daily basis Robinson came to understand and appreciate better the grinding poverty of the working class. His poetic horizons opened in new directions while his natural sympathy for the poor and unfortunate deepened.

Robinson's identification with the day laborers he met went beyond the work itself. He sought solace and relief from his woes in the saloon in just the same fashion as many of the other workers. The saloon had long been a target of the temperance movement. It symbolized iniquity, whereas to the men who patronized it the saloon was a place to forget the day just passed and to avoid worry about tomorrow. Opponents of traffic in liquor too often neglected the circumstances of drudgery and despair which drove many men to drink. Of all the social abuses which came under Progressive attack, drunkenness was least related by reformers to social conditions and more generally attributed to failure of character in the individual. Robinson, the well born New England Yankee, was no different from the impoverished and ignorant new American, in a desire to blot out reality by resort to whisky. Later, when the time came, he would be as resistant to the "noble experiment" of prohibition as any ethnic group in the metropolis, thereby adding to his identification with the city and its peoples.

Robinson could not have known it but the Fates were preparing a new destiny for him. In May of 1904 the first intimation of this occurred when the New York World published a heavy-handed human interest account, "A Poet of the Subway," the story of his days as a construction project worker. A piece of sensational reporting in keeping with the prescriptions of Joseph Pulitzer, Robinson himself greatly deplored what he saw as cheap publicity. But the story did dramatize the dilemma of an artist and popularized it as well. It was not likely to do harm and just possibly the newspaper account might contribute to an improvement in the fortunes of the subway poet.

Those fortunes took a sudden and unexpected turn for the better in 1904 when Robinson's work came to the attention of Theodore Roosevelt, then campaigning for his second term as president. The entire Roosevelt-Robinson episode has a story book appeal. It is, none-theless, an authentic vignette which well described one more turn of the wheel of fortune. Kermit Roosevelt, the President's son, was a student at Groton School where his hall master was Dick Richards of Gardiner, Maine. Among the books Richards kept was, not surprisingly, a copy of that slim volume of Robinson's verse, The Children of the Night. Kermit read the poems and liked many of them. Obtaining a copy for himself he had another sent to his father at the White House. Few presidents could have been as susceptible to the poetry of E.A. Robinson as was T.R. As the saying goes, "a

book a day" was part of life in the Roosevelt household,
a habit to which young and old alike were equally
attached. As for the President his range of literary
interests was impressive. He knew the Chanson de Roland
and the Nibelungenlied, but he was no less at home with
Shelley and Swinburne. He was quick to appreciate
Robinson's poetic accomplishment and his future
promise.16 Learning a little of Robinson from Richard
Watson Gilder, editor of The Century Magazine, the
President wrote directly to the poet. He told him that
he enjoyed the poems in The Children of the Night, "so
much so that I must write and tell you so." He went on.
"Will you permit me to ask what you are doing and how
you are getting along? I wish I could see you." The
letter was signed: "Sincerely yours, Theodore
Roosevelt." Clearly the President wanted to be of some
help and was in a position to do as much. When Gilder
became more fully apprised of Robinson's plight he wrote
Roosevelt, suggesting that "some minor appointment might
be given Robinson." Perhaps a consular position in
England would have been appropriate. Roosevelt was
against sending literary people abroad, however. He
felt that for Robinson to go to England, for example,
would be "the worst possible thing" because the creative
artist would be separated from the wellsprings of his
art. T.R.'s nationalism extended to culture as well as
politics, though he was no mere chauvinist in this
respect. The President was more than willing to assist.
Robinson declined to accept the first job offered him, a
position as immigration inspector in either Mexico or
Canada. T.R. responded by asking what kind of position
would be agreeable. Robinson put his problem very
plainly in a letter to a friend. "The trouble with me,"
he wrote, "is that I want to live in New York. I can't

feel at home anywhere else."17   And Robinson stuck to
his guns. Within a short time the President appointed
him "special agent" of the Treasury Department, working
at the New York Customs House at a salary of $2,000 a
year.   "I don't know a special agent of the Treasury
from the mother of Samson," he confided to Hays
Gardiner. "All I know is that it means two thousand a
year with plenty of time to do my work."18 For the next
four years Robinson remained a civil servant, though in
name only, as he was expected to perform no duties in
the position. The President was immensely pleased with
the situation even though it was perhaps the one real
occasion when he officially strayed from his tough Civil
Service code of ethics. Robinson for his part was
delighted. He was able to pay his debts, to offer
financial aid to his brother Herman's children, and to
put his personal life in some kind of order. And, as he
had remarked, he had plenty of time to devote to poetry.
It was a fair arrangement all around.

The poet had other reasons for feeling indebted to
the President. Not only had T.R. "discovered" him, he
also made some useful representations in Robinson's
behalf with a publishing house. This favor he carried
out with skill and a little arm twisting. He had been
eager to meet Robinson since reading The Children of the
Night and so contrived to have him visit Sagamore Hill
at a time when Robert Bridges, the literary advisor of
Charles Scribner's Sons, was present. The encounter was
an exciting one for Robinson who discovered in the
President that rich vein of literary ore lying just
below the surface of his public image. Soon after,
Scribner's brought out a new edition of The Children of
the Night. In August of 1905 there appeared in The

Outlook Roosevelt's fulsome review of the Robinson volume in which the President discovered, as he told his readers, "an undoubted touch of genius" in the poems.19 The passing years during which Robinson became an important poet were to show how handsomely he paid his debt to fortune.

A harder look at Robinson and Roosevelt together suggests that they had much more in common than a story-book friendship. Robinson and Roosevelt enjoyed what was a "common vision." Theodore Roosevelt represented the center position in the spectrum of American politics during the Progressive Era. It was, furthermore, a vital center as it combined both stability and movement. In Richard Hofstadter's apt phrase, Roosevelt was "the conservative as Progressive." Robinson, in turn, spoke the artistic response to the world about him which the Progressives were seeking to change for the better. Despite their different backgrounds and divergent experiences there were some unexpected and arresting convergences between the two men. A comparison of Roosevelt's public mind and certain of Robinson's "socio-historical" poetry demonstrated this common vision. Their spiritual affinity went well beyond the aestheticism of the creative artist echoing the public man's love of nature and his sponsorship of conservation legislation. It was a kinship drawing heavily on the American sense of mission, a feeling for its high destiny rooted in the national consciousness and mani-fested in its national history. And so coming to maturity in an America that was experiencing great material advances and concomitantly an alteration of its traditional moral commitment, neither poet nor president was left undisturbed by the advance of the new morality.

While it is an easy matter to point out that Robinson
and Roosevelt disagreed on certain large issues facing
the nation, of which American expansion overseas after
1898 is the most persuasive example, it is well to
emphasize that they possessed a common awareness of what
they considered the besetting illness of their times and
a common vision of what was needed to cure the illness.
They displayed a single reaction to what they both spoke
of as the materialization of American life, and in their
own ways they sought to make common cause against it.
Surely neither the poetic stature of Edwin Arlington
Robinson nor the historical reputation of Theodore
Roosevelt can be said to rest only on their opposition
to a fully materialized America. But just as certainly
the evidence of their opposition argues for the persis-
tence of a morally orthodox strain in the American
temper.

Both Robinson and Roosevelt were born to a tradition
of individualism, and for each of them it was an
individualism antithetical to the harsh postulates of
Herbert Spencer's Social Statics. It spoke of responsibility and service as integral parts of striving for
good. Their world was one of absolutes, not precisely
defined, but commanding their adherence nonetheless. In
so far as each managed to insist upon the individual's
integrity as the foundation of a sound political life,
as for life itself, their resolution of the problem of
man in society ought to be appreciated as emerging from
a congeries of contending and in some ways conflicting
moralities. For Robinson this inner contention included
a Puritan heritage which was real enough, traces and
more of Emerson and Royce, and the lessons offered by
the economic consolidations and scientific speculations

which were helping to shape America in the second half of the nineteenth century. Roosevelt's adherence to the old-fashioned individualism survived the assaults of Social Darwinism and the magnetic appeal for power for its own sake that for him was sometimes cloaked by American nationalism. The intellectual formation of these two men, when taken together, would seem to mirror their generation faithfully enough to view the results as portraying a significant portion of that generation's moral doubt and its idealized resolution.

Theodore Roosevelt was an enormously popular figure in his own time which is one good reason for viewing him as a general barometer of the public mood and outlook. Contemporaries applauded him for his zest for living and for his ability to accomplish much and historians have continued to speak of these years as the "era of Theodore Roosevelt." But his advocacy of the strenuous life even as he lived it should not be permitted to obscure or to detract from his vision. Behind action there lay principles, derived from an assessment of man that appeared to him at once as natural and workable and which appealed to the American people as worthwhile. This view was best expressed by T.R. when he spoke, as he often did, of the need of character in men's personal habits and in social life. His own definition of character needs little elaboration. "By character I mean the sum of qualities essential to moral efficiency. Among them are resolution, courage, energy, self-control, fearlessness in taking initiative, and in assuming responsibility, and a just regard for the rights of others." The value of character in the individual was quite transcendent, becoming "the foundation stone of national life." The place of character in

Roosevelt's thought is of especial value for understanding the nature and purpose of his Progressivism.
He proposed to reform America by reforming the
individual. At the very least he would reform the nation
by applying individual moral standards to corporate,
political and class behavior. The effort to reconcile
the place of character and the function of law as an
instrument designed to promote social betterment
Roosevelt well summarized in the following passage from
one of his 1912 campaign addresses. "We are not
proposing to substitute law for character. We are
merely proposing to buttress character by law. In civil
life it is the individual character which counts most;
in addition thereto there lie ready to hand the social
weapons which can be forged only by law and by public
opinion." All of this is a steadfast reminder of the
traditionalism of a Progressive president's moral world
and that of the American people who supported him.[20]

A like pattern is discernible in certain socio-
historical poems of Edwin Arlington Robinson.
Robinson's answers to the perplexities of life of whatever kind went straight to the individual. In these
poems he made use of figures and episodes drawn from
American history, or from the contemporary national
scene, to foil his moralizing. He rarely came to grips
with those peculiar concepts which are the stock-in-
trade of the sociologist, however, nor did he find it
congenial to reduce his criticism to "social significance." For him society before all else was composed of
men and women as individuals and the environment they
were placed in should not be thought of as necessarily
determining them in questions of right or wrong. Even in
his early years with their distinctly idealistic propen-

sities, Robinson did not bring himself to abandon the
world to its own devices. In a letter to Daniel Gregory
Mason, commenting on Thoreau's essay, "Walking," he
wrote:

> I stretched out yesterday and read
> "Walking", but did not quite relish what
> seemed to be to me a sort of glorified
> world-cowardice all through the thing.
> For God's sake, says the sage, let me get
> away into the wilderness where I shall
> not have a single responsibility or the
> first symptom of social discipline. Let
> me be a pickerel or a skunk cabbage, or
> anything that will not have to me the
> realities of civilization.21

For Robinson, personally, in even his incidental
dealings with people, "to do a little spiritual good in
the world" was the fuel which kept him going.22

The total of his verse likewise displayed a spiritual
concern. From the first songs of the fledgling muse to
the final dramas of the major poet, Robinson rarely
departed from the fundamental purpose of his art: to
reflect on and to interpret the meaning of life.
Robinson sought out man as might a scientist in the
laboratory, delineating him in his essential relationships. His was a dissection of man _qua_ man, usually
proposing to judge him as being ruled by a scheme of
spiritual values. The poetry resulting carried with it
a moral, it was fashioned out of ethical terms, and the
sanctions of the ethics were such as to give signifi-

cance to life. Robinson's criticisms of humanity were varied in content, they recorded his sustained struggle to come to a knowledge of life, and mirrored faithfully the influential elements in his background. Inherited traditionalism lost some of its immediacy when paralleled by the philosophical appeals of Emerson and Royce, while scientific skepticism introduced a quality of doubt that was with Robinson to the last. On balance, however, Robinson sought to give expression to a humanized ethic which in many ways was redolent of an ancient faith.

As though to supply a convenient guide to his awareness of the American dream and the troubles it had encountered in its search for fulfillment, Robinson wrote a series of interpretative poetic sketches of figures prominent in American history. These constituted settings for the statement of certain of his sociopolitical convictions which were especially germane to the Progressive mood and purpose. While in one sense his moral precepts need not be thought of as confined to any one national experience, still America was his country and he was deeply aware of it. As with Theodore Roosevelt, Lincoln was an outstanding hero to Robinson. He saw in Lincoln "The Master," a spokesman of a great moral cause, the leader of a nation enduring its moment of agony in order that men and women might be free.[23] What were the qualities he discovered in Lincoln? Leadership, he wrote, asks meekness and patience, endurance and humility. Lincoln became the "Titan" of his time, possessing these virtues in full measure. Robinson's moral reflexes may be gauged further by his estimation of John Brown at Harper's Ferry.[24] He was undoubtedly attracted to the wild idealism of Brown --

"there was a time for service and he served" -- yet he
judged the humanity of Lincoln as the more effective
cure of the curse of slavery than the violence of the
abolitionists.

Robinson possessed a kind of Hamiltonian faith in
democracy. In "On The Way" he wrote of an imaginary
dialogue between Hamilton and Aaron Burr.[25] Burr was
presented as an adventurer and an opportunist, annoyed
both by Washington's regal manner and by the incongruity
of a people ruling itself. How "are men to dance/ When
all men are musicians?" he wondered. Burr whispered
overtures to Hamilton to join him in a half-hatched plot
to gain power but Hamilton turned temptation aside. "We
are done with ermine," Hamilton insisted. Yet
Hamilton's decision was made to appear as resting as
much on faith in Washington's leadership as in his trust
of the people. And so it was with Robinson. He felt
that leadership in democracy, and in particular in a
democratic government needing reform, as was the case of
the United States at the beginning of the twentieth
century, was indispensable. The poem, "The Revealer,"
which was dedicated to Theodore Roosevelt, conveyed this
thought in a manner akin to T.R.'s own pronouncements.[26]
In the poem Robinson argued that the need for democratic
leadership was great, yet it was limited by the nature
of democracy. It was the function of the leader under
such circumstances to reveal to his fellow citizens the
mistakes and attendant evils in public policy:" ... the
combs of long defended hives/ ... dishonored and
unclean." For a free people, however, reform of abuses
rested finally with the citizens. The leader could only
serve as a conscience-guide. It was the people who had
to act.

What you and I and Anderson
Are still to do is his reward,
If we go back when he is gone --
There is an Angel with a Sword.[27]

The lesson was meant to be clear. The effectiveness of a leader in a democracy was finally determinedby the willingness of the people to follow where he took them. This was a recognition of the role the people must act out in the continuing process of moral renewal which was the preliminary to public renewal. Yet all this implied that the people must be capable somehow of a constructive reaction to a leader; otherwise the leadership of the kind described in "The Revealer" had little relevance. For President Roosevelt these ideas were summed up in what he called "the Lincoln School" of American politics. By this he meant a government strong and efficient in the Hamiltonian style, but Jeffersonian in a belief that the people were the ultimate authority and that the welfare of the people was the end of government. These were propositions which described the broad center of the Progressive Movement and which have made it appear to some as a liberal reform and to others as highly conservative. For a poet ordinarily thought of as remote from the immediacy of political life Robinson had made some acute observations and judgments, seemingly joining Roosevelt as a "conservative Progressive."

"The Revealer" was the final poem in a collection, The Town Down The River, which was published in 1910 and dedicated to Theodore Roosevelt. Many of the other poems were reminders of Robinson's life in New York.

"The White Lights (Broadway, 1906)" described the city
as having "triumph in the air," even though everyday men
and women had much of fear and wonder in their lives
there.[28]   In "Bon Voyage," perhaps in reference to himself, Robinson described his hero as a "Child of the
Cyclades/ And of Broadway," acknowledging the inheritance of Greece and the spirit of the contemporary age.[29]
Few places in New York did Robinson know better than the
saloons, so that "Calverly's" bespoke a mood stolen
directly from their atmosphere.[30]   In this poem man's
uncertain destiny was stressed -- perhaps he was "Lost
among the stars."   Robinson sounded a more hopeful note
in the title poem, "The Town Down The River," despite
lines such as "where millions cringe and shiver."[31]
This thought was authentic to the poet because he was
bound to be honest when he attempted to evaluate life's
experiences.   He was able, nonetheless, to find in the
city lights which were shining amidst the gloom.   The
pursuit of truth was part of his perennial dilemma in
facing life, whether in its larger or its more circum-
scribed dimensions.   The pursuit of truth was
substituted, in a very real way, for the old faith.
Other intellectuals of his time, among them William
Graham Sumner, had much the same attitude, that the
search for truth was special to man, in keeping with the
scientific spirit of continuing inquiry.   Robinson went
beyond Sumner, in fact, to Malebranche who insisted that
Truth was the peculiar possession of God while Man's
mission was the pursuit of Truth.   For Robinson, while
complete knowledge of the Divine remained outside human
attainment, at times it appeared only just beyond his
reach.   His nearness to the unattainable made his
dilemma especially poignant.   In no poem in The Town
Down The River was the problem of the artist more

sharply etched than in the popular "Miniver Cheevy."32
Miniver Cheevy was drawn to the past as he dreamed of
Thebes and Camelot. He disliked the present, cursing
the commonplace. But the crux of his difficulty was
that he "scorned the gold he sought/ But sore annoyed
was he without it." This was a succinct rendering of
the dynamic which motivated much of Robinson's commentary on mankind's search for happiness.

These poems and many others in The Town Down The
River emphasized the highly personal nature of Edwin
Arlington Robinson's art. They were starkly introspective at times, indicative that during these years
Robinson had not had an easy time in getting beyond
himself. His immediate experiences were paramount. The
world was there but he tended to neglect it quite as
much as the world neglected him. The people he wrote
about -- Clavering, Leffingwell, Uncle Ananias and their
troubles -- were real enough though they might seem to
be suspended in time and space. Occasionally these
characters were fitted out with the clothing of wider
appeal; more often they stood for no more than
Robinson's personal projections of Everyman. Many of
the poems in The Town Down The River were not so much
disappointing as they were limited. Robinson had to
work his way out of his personal world slowly, as a
consideration of his next collection, The Man Against
The Sky, published six years later amply shows. But
until the appearance of Merlin in 1917 he did not appear
to have broken clear of the circle of self to make a
difference for his poetry. This movement away from self
paralleled Robinson's own life after he left the Customs
House job in 1909.

The loss of the government sinecure was but one minor instance of a general redistribution of patronage usual to a new president in office. William Howard Taft, elected in 1908, was politician enough to have his own views as to how the political plums should be passed out. Theodore Roosevelt had done as much when he succeeded McKinley in 1901, though the latter had not harbored a poet on the civil list. Robinson was especially vulnerable to dismissal because T.R. had seen to it that he was to do no work at all. In any event Robinson found it possible to fall back on friends once again, whether in New York, Boston, or the New England countryside. He was encouraged by the prospect that a new book of poems was in press, evidence that he had used his Customs House job to good effect. Still he needed income, feeling responsibility for his sister-in-law and his young nieces. Offered a chance to tutor he turned that down and instead tried his hand at writing a novel. A best-selling novel became an illusion under which he lived briefly. His idea was to alter and add to Van Zorn, one of two plays he had written some years before. He spent most of the summer of 1910 working on the novel which was supposed to dispel his financial worries forever, but nothing came of it. Poetry again proved to be his true métier.

Robinson's reluctance to take a paying job after leaving the Customs House did not mean that he intended to revert to the derelict condition of the years prior to 1905. He had gained a new respect for himself and a new stability of outlook, despite or because of being on the government dole. His receipt of regular income stirred certain of his bourgeois prejudices which combined with a pride of realization that someone as powerful and as respected as Roosevelt was his friend and patron. Robinson, having gained a certain fame by association, was comfortable with his newfound reputation. Not yet recognized as a major poet he no longer went unnoticed, which was somewhat remarkable for one who had been anonymous for so long. In addition there were old friends to rely on and new friends to brighten his life, people who loved both the poet and the man. By 1910, while the dilemma of the artist continued unabated, the dilemma of survival was never again to be a factor in his life. Of the various elements which went to explain the new Robinson perhaps none was more important than his discovery of the MacDowell Colony for Artists, though it would be more accurate to say that the Colony discovered him. Founded by Mrs. Edward Mac-Dowell in memory of her husband, the composer and musician, in Peterborough, New Hampshire the Colony was just then beginning to establish a reputation as a retreat for creative people in the arts. Robinson had an instinctive aversion from "artists' colonies" they connoted to him a gathering place for dilettantes, mortal enemies of true art. But MacDowell was different, argued Hermann Hagedorn who was well acquainted with the character of the Colony and believed it a likely place for Robinson to write.33

Had Robinson been employed as a Treasury Agent when Hagedorn suggested that he spend the summer of 1911 at Peterborough, he would have rejected the idea. He would have said, and rightly so perhaps, that his "duties" in the civil service made it necessary for him to remain in New York. Bowing to Hagedorn's insistence and having no good excuse for not doing so, Robinson agreed to give the MacDowell Colony a try. As he soon discovered the

Colony was the near perfect contrapuntal note to the
city in his life. He was at ease and happy at Peterborough almost from the outset, in so far as he was ever
comfortable except with his closest friends. Every
summer from 1911 to 1934, his last, Robinson enjoyed the
quiet inspiration of the MacDowell Colony.

Edwin Arlington Robinson was, in the phrase of Henry
James, "that queer monster, the artist, an obstinate
finality, and inexhaustible sensibility." Typically, he
was interested in finalities, bringing to them sensibility of a high order. MacDowell was to help in the
further definition of Robinson, the artist. He took
there with him his determination to possess no more of
the world than was truly essential to him to describe,
as best he could, the final purpose of man in the
cosmos. The great bulk of Robinson's work lay ahead.
Both the range and the quality of his output grew out of
his altered life style, in which MacDowell was a key
element. There was a time to suffer and a time to
write. Robinson's time to write was at hand. He was
aware of what the Colony meant to him, and what it had
done for him. To show his gratitude, to Mrs. MacDowell
especially, he said that there was nothing left for him
but "to do the best work that is in me."[34] At the same
time he foreswore his old friend, the bottle. From 1916
to 1935 Robinson wrote sixteen major poems or collect-
ions of poems, averaging almost a major work a year,
beginning with The Man Against the Sky.

The declaration of faith, however non-theological it
was, which he made in The Children of the Night Robinson
again professed in "The Man Against The Sky."[35] Its
terms strongly connoted the universality of his vision.

The poem had a sense of anguish about it which was especially true to Robinson's state of mind when he wrote it. But hope purified the suffering state of man. Despite its abstractions "The Man Against The Sky" retained those personal elements which are so much a part of humanism. Once again the proper study of mankind was shown to be man. Cosmology aside, there were passages in "The Man Against The Sky" which were clearly expressions of the conviction that responsibility for human behavior was integral to a scheme of human values. It had something of a mystery-inflected religious component in lines like:

> And we ....
> Must each await alone at his own height
> Another darkness or another light.[36]

The stress was placed not on social concern but on individual guilt. In his poetry, as in his letters, Robinson was reluctant to construe the nature of eternal sanctions. He persisted, however, in his belief that if life meant anything, some kind of moral price must be exacted.

"The Man Against The Sky" was a complete and moving expression of E.A. Robinson's anti-materialism. To Hermann Hagedorn he remarked: "If materialism is true, then parenthood is assuredly the greatest of all crimes and the sooner the much advertized `race' is annihilated the better. But you know my own opinions and therefore you know I am not a materialist. As a matter of fact," he concluded, "I suppose that I'm the damnedest optimist that ever lived."[37] Anti-materialism had been the primary motivation for Robinson in writing "The Man

Against The Sky." In the poem he was particularly
caustic in detailing the several claims which science
had made regarding the nature of man and his destiny.
Thescientist, and his attempt to build "A living reason
out of molecules," he scorned because the scientist only
saw "with his shrewd mechanic eyes/ A world without
meaning."[38] Robinson attacked "the pretensions of the
new gospel" of infant science, irrespective of their
social or individual application. He accepted nothing
of the laws of science as germane to a resolution of
man's moral problems. This same note rang persistently
through Robinson's later work and is commonly discerned
as part of the optimism which, granting the world to be
a "hell of a place," as he remarked to Hagedorn, was in
reality the explanation of his perennial hope.[39] His
private comments on the meaning of "The Man Against The
Sky" further stressed its anti-materialism. "My purpose
was to cheer people up and incidentally to indicate the
futility of materialism as a thing to live by," he told
Louis Ledoux.[40] To Amy Lowell he was no less explicit.
"Nothing could have been farther from my mind when I
wrote `The Man' than any emissary of gloom or despair.
In the closing lines I meant, through what I supposed to
be an obvious ironic medium, to carry materialism to its
logical end and to indicate its futility as an explanation or justification for existence."[41]

Respecting materialism, rarely was Robinson's attitude more forcefully expressed on any important subject
as in his private letters. On no other aspect of his
outlook did he appear to be more convinced from first to
last, from his early "Credo," to "The March of the
Cameron Men," published in 1932. In writing Hays
Gardiner shortly after the publication of The Children

of the Night he took issue with the methods of William James, for example, arguing that the pragmatist "does not seem to see that Spencer's philosophy includes his own, for what it is worth," and that to agree with James was to accept Spencer's materialism.[42] This same criticism he applied to the materialism of Will Durant in a detailed refutation written from Peterborough in 1931. "The cocksureness of the modern `mechanist' means nothing to me; and I doubt if it means any more to him when he pauses really to think." "But if life is only what it appears to be," he argued in another way, "no amount of improvement or enlightenment will ever compensate or atone for what it has inflicted and endured in ages past, or for what it is inflicting or enduring today."[43] As for his great poem, "The Man Against The Sky," it is correct to observe that in it Robinson had packed his mature conclusions and while he saw no reason to repeat them he discovered continued justification for exploring them further.

III

WAR AND DEMOCRACY

With the onset of the twentieth century the Western World had been propelled to new heights of material well-being by the twin engines of science and technology. Continued want and misery, of which there remained no small amount, were so many were challenges to be met, so many problems to be solved. America was especially favored by the fruits of man's genius and labor under the dual sign of capitalism and republicanism at a time when the Progressive reformers sought to orchestrate the tunes of profit and self-government into new and satisfying harmonies. America and Europe seemed in phase in all this, a promise of sustained betterment for the advanced nations of the world. One statesman summed it up as "the world movement of superior peoples." If it bred a complacency about the end of war as an instrument of international politics among the Great Powers, this was nevertheless a conviction widely held. There was plenty of evidence in the decade and a half before 1914 that war was not only possible but likely, given the nationalistic impulse, and the system of alliances and scramble for empire which were its offspring. But general war, nonetheless, had become "unthinkable." That the outbreak of World War I shattered this illusion and scattered the pieces across the breadth of the world and the length of the twentieth century merits little amplification here. Contemporaries and historians alike have made the point and expounded its corollaries in

countless ways. Nationalism had proved to be the over-
mastering force at work in the world and in the lives of
individuals. The response of the masses and the classes
to the call to arms in 1914 was overwhelming. Men of
letters and science were by no means found wanting.
James Bryce, Regius Professor of Civil Law at Oxford,
was ready to wage as ruthless a war with his pen as
Tommy Atkins was expected to fight in the trenches. The
Academie Française knew instinctively what every
Frenchman must do to defend la patrie against another
German army marching on Paris, while nearly one hundred
leading German professors and writers published an
"appeal to the civilized world" in praise of German war
aims.

Three thousand miles of ocean insulated America from
this initial burst of passion. To the average American
the war meant little. American reaction stood as a
pointed reminder of just how removed people felt from
the affairs of the Old World, the European cockpit.
Highly informed Americans were cautious or neutral.
Oliver Wendell Holmes, Jr., while he regretted the
devastating effects which the conflict was sure to have
on Great Britain, at the same time expressed the view
that the destruction of a cultured and civilized Germany
was also lamentable. President Wilson enunciated both
the official policy and the subconscious feelings of the
country when he urged a strict neutrality. Even the
vibrant Theodore Roosevelt, who before long would be in
the vanguard of those demanding United States entry into
the war, took the position that the fate of Belgium was
tied to the fact that when giants collided pygmy nations
must expect to be trampled on. "Poor little Belgium"
was still to be born in the mind of the propagandist.

Yet the fact of a general war in Europe posed problems for the American intellectual and artist alike. The intellectual who had assumed the operational values of science and technology faced the prospect of a world brought down rather than lifted up. The artist, grounding his work in sensitivity and aspiration, saw these human qualities blunted and still worse for him, prostituted in the name of the nation state.[1]

E.A. Robinson experienced both the pangs of intellectual anguish and the disillusionment of artistic purpose in his contemplation of the Great War. The poem, "Cassandra,"[2] which was typical of his distress over the materialism of society, grew from his deepening realization of the causes of the war and its probable outcome. "He was appalled by the easy optimism of the average American, the cheap idealism, the faith in phrases and gestures, the waves of fear and greed, the spiritual inadequacy to meet the challenge of world catastrophe," according to Hermann Hagedorn who was very close to him in these days.[3] The war, thought Robinson, was the product of rampant materialism on a personal as on an imperial scale. He leveled his criticisms not simply at nations but at individuals whose cumulative materialism, as translated by modern economic practice into war for markets and political hegemony, had brought about the chaos of a world war. Robinson stressed the fact of individual responsibility for what the economist termed pressures or the sociologist forces. As he wrote in "Cassandra,"

> Your Dollar is your only Word
> The wrath of it your only fear.[4]

This was a cry of alarm against the bitch-goddess, Success, which too many Americans had put in place of God. What had happened in America was a domestication of materialism as it grew from the Gilded Age to leviathan stature in the twentieth century. Robinson accentuated this with the following lines.

> "Your Dollar, Dove and Eagle make
> a Trinity that even you
> Rate higher than you rate yourselves.
> It pays, it flatters and it's new.

> "And though your very flesh and blood
> Be what your Eagle eats and drinks
> You'll praise him for the best of birds
> Not knowing what the Eagle thinks."[5]

This scathing description of Americans and America in "Cassandra" Robinson chose to close with a question, which amounted to an accusation.

> "Think you to tread forever down
> The merciless old verities,
> Are you never to have eyes
> To see the world for what it is?"[6]

The entry of the United States into World War I in 1917 became somewhat incidental to the larger moral problem of the Western World, as Robinson judged the matter. With very few exceptions American scholars and intellectuals were ready to support this new departure, Wilsonian idealism. Wilson was, after all, an intellectual in politics. Progressive professors, like Charles A. Beard at Columbia University, university presidents, like John Grier Hibben of Princeton, who stated the case for military training at colleges and universities, and philosophers, John Dewey among them, found it relatively easy to jump on the martial bandwagon in imitation of their Old World counterparts. Nationalism was endemic to the Western World. Dewey's enthusiasms for the war was among the most puzzling. In Creative Intelligence, which he had brought out in early 1917, he had asserted that the scientific method and not force must be the means utilized to better man's condition.[7] When the United States went to war, however, Dewey went along. Not only did he argue for a justification of force to bring about an equitable and lasting peace, he wrote further that the socialization of the means of production which must be part of any war effort would simply hasten the day when government would be accepted as the appropriate manager of an increasingly complex society. War was consistent with the utility principle implicit in pragmatism, which worked to make this war a good and useful thing.

Little enough dissent from America's new role as a combatant was heard from the intellectual community. Randolph Bourne appeared like a host of one, contending that "an intellectual class that was wholly rational would have to call insistently for peace and not for war." But his protests had small effect.[8] Jane Addams, who had spoken out strongly against the war when it began in 1914, was equally opposed to war as an instrument of public policy as the United States entered the conflict in 1917. When she tried to explain her position in "Patriotism and Pacifism in Wartime," an address she frequently gave, a once admiring public rejected her and her views.[9] The Christian churches,

not to be outdone, supported American involvement
readily enough. Rev. John Burke, writing in The
Catholic World, rather typically issued "a call to
patriotism," pronouncing the war "eminently just."[10]
E.A. Robinson was as depressed as a man might be at this
mounting evidence of the Spenglerian thesis playing
itself to a conclusion, yet he was not totally lacking
in patriotic sentiment himself. As the battles of 1918
went forward he confessed to one friend that he felt he
"ought to be driving a mule in France," while admitting
to a "feeling of insufficiency in wartime."[11] Age and
temperament, in any event, had dictated otherwise,
though the war was to have a definite influence on his
art.

Robinson's war-time poetry displayed a distinctive
quality. As with many intellectuals the war signified
to him the end of an old order in the larger affairs of
men and the introduction of a new and uncertain era.
Force had become the "ultimate ratio" in the lives of
nations as in the lives of individuals. Robinson had
concluded well in advance of 1917 that personal moral
responsibility was being overwhelmed by scientific
determinism and with it came the notion of impermanent
values in society. The World War magnified this in a
gruesome and catastrophic way. The world had slipped
its moorings, portending the doom of things as men had
known them for generations. Robinson was aghast at what
he saw. He proposed to speak out in two major poems,
Merlin and Lancelot. These works were products not
alone of the war years but directly of the war. The
dilemma of the artist, in fact, had become so acute that
Robinson could not deal with it except by resort to a
kind of subterfuge. He proposed to retreat from a world

gone mad to another time, more orderly, more predictable, and more to his liking. In the medieval era,
which was the setting for <u>Merlin</u> and <u>Lancelot</u>, the
distinction between right and wrong was not blurred by
science. The rules of conduct were absolute and were
understood. The disarray of contemporary society had
caused the poet to yearn for another, more stable time
wherein he might place a cast of characters and allow
them to wrestle with good and evil, the sanctions of the
moral law emerging as an operative factor. The
symbolism of these poems, which Robinson consciously
intended, was without meaning unless there was an
acceptance of common beliefs. It was a symbolism which
certainly would have held a different clue to Robinson's
mind had he chosen to use any other historical period.
The symbolism of the kingdom of Camelot, "doomed
Camelot," was that of the decline of the Western World,
yet not cast completely in Spenglerian terms. As
Robinson wrote in his own reflection on the meaning of
<u>Merlin</u>, "You may still call me an evangel of ruin ...
but you must not forget the redemption -- even if you
don't see it."[12] Robinson refused to write off the
Western World completely. Mankind might still be
redeemable, though in the midst of World War I it was a
dubious prospect.

The characters of the Arthurian pieces were not the
stock-in-trade of chivalry. Instead they were men and
women, highly individualized, yet universal in their
appeal. It was in their universality and in the establishment of a positive and absolute ethical norm on such
a scale that we are given an understanding of Robinson's
traditionalism. Through the moral values which guided
the lives of these characters the verities as Robinson

construed them were justly stated. This is why <u>Merlin</u>
and <u>Lancelot</u> were part of the poet's response to the
dilemma of the artist contemplating the meaning of the
World War. At the same time the poems included a full
expression of the philosophical basis for principles
toward which Robinson had been building from his earlier
work.

Over and above the symbolism of the particular characters, action in these two poems was suggestive of the
circumstances in which the figures moved. There was the
symbolism of the decline of the American character due
to its abandonment of morality, a "half-realized vision
of the Holy Grail." Robinson stood apart from his times
in an attempt to allegorize the age and thereby to speak
a warning of impending disaster unless his countrymen
became aware of the inadequacies of science when applied
to morality. This was more important, in fact, than the
figure of Camelot for a doomed world because it identified the root cause of the doom. The sins upon which
Camelot was built suggested the sin of materialism
generally, upon which the modern phase of Western
culture was grounded.

The poem, <u>Merlin</u>, was the particular statement of
Camelot.[13] Camelot had been made a kingdom by the
wizard, Merlin, and he had made Arthur king. A man of
ungovernable passion, Arthur begot the bastard, Mordred.
Merlin meanwhile had become enamored of the lovely
Vivian and took her for his pleasure. As the years
passed Mordred, the child of sin, plotted the ruin of
Camelot in hopes of seizing power for himself. The
tragedy of Camelot deepened when Arthur's passion
settled on Guinevere, already loved by Lancelot. The

king was aware of Lancelot's love but he was determined
to have his way. Lancelot fled the court to save
Guinevere. This defection by the noblest of Arthur's
knights only hastened the doom of Camelot. According to
Merlin, it was Mordred,the offspring of Arthur's sin,
who conspired the ruin of the kingdom. Both the wizard
and the king were profoundly disturbed. In consequence
of all this Merlin was led to abandon Vivian and to
return to the king's side. Even so, he knew he could
not avert the doom of Camelot. He was "neither Fate nor
God." In Merlin's words, Camelot was a

> "...kingdom builded on two pits
> Of Living Sin, - so founded by
>   the will
> Of one wise counselor who loved
>   the king
> And loved the world and therefore
>   made him king
> To be a mirror for it, - the king
>   reigned well
> For certain years, awaiting a sure
>   doom;
> For certain years he waved across
>   the world
> A royal banner with a Dragon on it;
> And men of every land fell worshipping
> The Dragon as if it were the living God,
> And not the living sin."[14]

This heavy sense of sin in _Merlin_ demonstrated at once
that Robinson concerned himself with an objective moral
order, the reality of which was central to the impending
doom of Camelot. Personal sin implied, furthermore, the

personal responsibility of free men. At the same time
it presupposed the larger Christian-inspired scheme of
redemption. Arthur knew he had sinned. He said to
Merlin: "... I have sinned and erred and heeded not/Your
counsel ....'"[15] He realized as well that he had built
his life on "`sand and mud, and shall see no Grail.'"[16]
Remorse of conscience here was concerned with personal
sanctions to which the individual must submit. But the
symbolism to be effective required more, and received it
in the words of Arthur's self-description:

> "... a king who built his palaces
> On sand and mud, and hears them
>   crumbling now,
> And sees them tottering, as he
>   knew they must."[17]

Individual sin, in short, carried with it social
consequences.

True to her figuration of the world and its ways,
Vivian was unable to find in Arthur's sin either
personal blame or cosmic implications. She doubted the
relevance to Merlin and to her of an act which some men
called sin. She asked, in fear of losing Merlin, "Why
all this new insistence upon sin?"[18] Merlin's reply
spoke his mind. He reprimanded Vivian for her failure
to be aware of the wages of sin, saying that the ill
effects of the king's action were such that all men
surely were alive to them:

> "... There is no man, or any woman,
> For whom the story of the living king
> Is not the story of the living sin.

> I thought my story was the common one,
> For common recognition and regard."[19]

To Merlin, in his merely worldly wisdom, sin was the
beginning of the troubles of Camelot, and symbolically
for Robinson it was at the root of a disintegrating
world. Sin, in fact, was the essential abstraction in
Merlin. Rather than attempt to define sin beyond the
requirements of the story of Merlin Robinson preferred
to speak of a sense of sin, a lack of personal moral
integrity and the dire consequences of this for others
in society. He consciously intended the poem as an
object lesson to prove to future generations that
nothing can hope to stand on a rotten foundation. It
was a "moral for the speckled ages."[20] As Robinson
wrote Hagedorn, "the most significant line in the two
poems [Merlin and Lancelot] considered from a purely
practical point of view is, perhaps, `The world has paid
enough for Camelot'."[21]

Granting as much, it is hard to avoid the impression that Fate pervaded Robinson's story of Merlin to a
striking degree. This sense of the inevitable can be
related in a way to the determination which was part of
his Social Darwinist inheritance, and against which he
tended to struggle:

> "that all your certainties have
>   bruises on `em
> All your pestilent asseverations
> Will never make a man a salamander."[22]

Merlin gave Fate a genuine primacy: "`On Fate there is
novengeance even for God.'"[23] The imputation of

fatalism was there, a half disguised reminder of the dilemma of many American artists in a modern, scientific society.

Merlin and Lancelot[24] were two sides of the one coin of moral obligation. They should be read together, as Robinson tells us, not simply as part of the same epic but as having complementary values.[25] The sin of Merlin demanded the Light of Lancelot. The symbolism of the former was sustained in the latter in the struggle between good and evil, between right and wrong, which was central to the drama in Lancelot. Robinson's human beings suffered as human beings, because of sin, and when the transgressions were those of a king society suffered. But man conquered through faith, through an undeviating adherence to the Gleam, the Light. The Gleam of Lancelot, although it was an absolute idea for Robinson, was not presented as an absolute attraction for the knight. In the end it prevailed but only after a genuine conflict within Lancelot's soul. He was not a puppet, but someone who proposed to follow the Light after the fashion of a human decision. It was Lancelot's faith in the meaning of the Gleam which was absolute. Its effects on his life, once the decision was taken, were described in such a way as to suggest the supernatural. In general, all the characters in Lancelot accepted the cosmic certainty of the Light. Robinson made no provision for scoffers.

The thrust of Lancelot was, however, not to be found in the variety of acknowledgements of the reality of a mystic faith. It was in the struggle within an epic character for ascendency between the Light and another force. The opposing force was Lancelot's love

for Guinevere. The strength of this love was great.
Elements of divine Light and earthly love ordained the
contest. What was the Light that led Lancelot away from
the world at great personal sacrifice? Guinevere said,
and Lancelot agreed, it was not any worldly light, nor
was it the voice of the Church.[26] It appeared, instead,
as a unique and ethereal Gleam from "another world,"
"nor one that we may name."[27] This Light was the Grail
of the <u>Morte</u> <u>d'Arthur</u> given a psychological figure. But
it was still mystic and still miracle-working. Robinson
in his private correspondence wrote that the Light of
Lancelot was "simply the light of the Grail, interpreted
universally as a spiritual realization of things and
their significance."[28] An aversion to metaphysics would
permit Robinson no more concrete expression of it than
"one we may not name." But to understand the dilemma of
the artist requires that emphasis be placed on the
conflicting values of love and the Light. The point of
the poem was not so much a definition of the nature of
the Light -- though it was clearly a spiritual Something
-- as it was the dilemma of Lancelot, not unlike
Robinson's own troubled years when he was torn between
writing poetry and "getting a job." For Lancelot, as
for Robinson, the final victory was achieved by sacrifice. In Lancelot's case, it required Guinevere to
allow Lancelot to follow the Gleam, no less than it
demanded of the knight the will to continue to seek
after the Light. In following the Gleam and thus put-
ting the world aside Lancelot acted out of knowledge of
self, of self-awareness, one of the poet's favorite
standards of measurement. Lancelot's sacrifice was that
of no ordinary mortal. He represented epic-man and his
experience was of a universal kind. Robinson did not
state in so many words that the social order was to be

preserved by personal integrity on the part of all men because his first concern was for art, not philosophy or politics. But in the perspective of Merlin and Lancelot as a single moral thesis, this was his intention. Lancelot completed the allegory of a world which must be based on absolute principles if it was to survive.

Robinson had been deeply troubled by the World War. "Cassandra," Merlin, and Lancelot were poems that spoke his grave concern. Could he have been indifferent, much less unaware, of the search for peace which began almost as soon as the fighting itself and which was to continue after the war's end? As America committed itself to the ordeal of battle it simultaneously committed itself to winning a just peace. In Woodrow Wilson's thinking it was to be a "peace without victory." Wilsonian idealism swept across the country in 1919 and 1918 as Wilson himself was to sweep across the nation in his daring appeal in the summer of 1919, the political gamble which cost him his health and the fulfillment of his states-manlike vision of an end to war. To suggest that Wilson's dream of a peace made permanent by American membership in the League of Nations was analogous to Lancelot's pursuit of the Light would be to extrapolate beyond the evidence in either Robinson's poetry or letters. The parallel has a certain appeal, nonethe-less. Robinson, writing Lancelot in 1917, after the United States had entered the war, could not have been ignorant of the various plans which had been put forth and discussed and all of which looked to a reconstructed international order based on an association of nations. There were several such plans in the wind. In all likelihood America would have a major role to play in establishing world peace. Robinson himself has remarked on the salvation elements in <u>Merlin</u>. In <u>Lancelot</u>, in contrast, the salvation idea was written large enough for all to see and it required no special pleading. As sensitive as the poet was to the terrors of war he would have been in a way especially consistent with his temper and outlook, even more sensitive to the entreaties for peace. With America in the war the United States and her allies believed that victory and peace were but a matter of time. An end of the killing would mean there was still a chance to save Western Civilization. "Doomed Camelot" might yet be rescued. If no explicit analogy was made in either the poem or the poet's correspondence the temptation persists to remember Robinson as reflecting the hopes of mankind for a new world order as he unfolded his story of Lancelot and the knight's pursuit of the Light.[29]

The final American rejection in March of 1920 of the Versailles Treaty and with it League membership lowered one curtain and raised another. Wilsonian idealism had failed to achieve its objectives. In the wake of that failure came the Roaring Twenties. Robinson expressed himself at some length on these and related matters in a letter to Mabel Dodge Stern. With America absent from the League he thought it was likely to become a plaything "while Germany is getting herself and Russia together, for another grand smash." "You will see from this," he added, "that I have no faith in any social scheme that doesn't see beyond a moonshine millennium."[30] In "The Garden of the Nations"(1923)[31] Robinson maintained his gloomy course. The source of his worry was once again "the old worm of evil at the root." The second of the two stanzas of the poem was particularly incisive.

And when we are all gone, shall
  mightier seeds
And scions of a warmer spring put
  forth
A bloom and fruitage of a larger
  worth
  if, by chance
Or by approved short sight, more
  numerous weeds
And weevils be the next inheritance!

In the same letter to Mable Dodge Stern, Robinson wrote
what might be taken as an uncanny anticipation of the
political mood of the 1920's which yielded the "Demos
poems." He "wonder[ed] if it would take much to set me
yelling for an absolute monarchy in the country,
assuming that we haven't got one." At which point he
let the string out altogether. "The world is a hell of
a place; and if life and the universe mean anything,
there is no reason to suppose that it will ever be anything else. This, as I understand it, is the true
optimism."[32] Indeed, Robinson was in an uncharacter-
istically candid frame of mind at this time. He wrote
to Percy Mackaye that he was a democrat "in that I'm as
likely to form a life-long friendship with a coal-heaver
as with a millionaire (rather more so in fact)" but his
democracy ended there.[33] It was a lament not infre-
quently heard in any democratic age so that what is
significant about it is that Robinson showed himself
disturbed by the direction American democracy appeared
to be taking. The future under democracy was very much
on his mind both as an American and as an artist. "And
as for the democratization of art, there ain't no such

animal." he wrote. "Art may die, having served its
purpose, but it will never be popular. The bare bones
of great music will always hold the crowd, but they
won't know what it is that holds them. We poor devils
of poets must face the probability that there will never
be more than one person in a thousand who will know or
really care about poetry."[34] It was with such misgivings that E.A. Robinson peered uneasily into the
Twenties.

The election in 1920 of a mid-Western, small town
Republican, Warren G. Harding, under the banner of
normalcy spoke a disdain and a suspicion of former
allies and enemies alike.[35] "They borrowed the money,
didn't they!" -- President Coolidge's famous retort to
the Allied suggestion for scaled down war debts -- was
an apt statement of the spirit of isolation which
engulfed American thinking and which did not break down
in any substantial way until the eve of World War II.
Within the nation, meanwhile, normalcy began to define
itself through events and personalities, and through
policies and their implementation. The decade got off
to a forbidding start. Bombs and riots were the order
of the day. Disputes in the coal and steel industries
caused almost as much consternation as the Boston Police
Strike. The result was an hysteria which threatened to
break over into all areas of national life. In the face
of the Red Scare the superpatriot was soon demanding a
101% Americanism, a cloak thrown over a demand for
social conformity. Both Gopher Prairie and Middletown
expected their citizens to be much alike. To deviate
was to risk being branded a Bolshevik, easily the
dirtiest word in the new political rhetoric. Intoler-
ance assumed a variety of forms. Race riots singled out

the black minority as lynch law prevailed in most Southern states. Catholics and Jews came under the lash of the Ku Klux Klan. The objectives of the Klan were stated fiercely in its Constitution: "to unite white male persons, native born Gentiles, citizens of the United States of America, who owe no allegiance of any nature to a foreign power ... and thus to maintain the distinctive institutions, rights, privileges, principles, traditions, and ideals of a pure America." Some of the foregoing philosophy was translated into the Immigration Act of 1924 which discriminated against future immigrants from eastern and southern Europe.

Accompanying the new conformity was the paradox of a more tolerant morality. The sense of purpose common to the war gave way to a self-indulgence, demanding its own conformity. Skirts were raised as morals were lowered. Free love, perhaps more talked about than practiced, became a period symbol. Religion of the conventional kind seemed to offer too little antidote to the new morality. Indeed science enjoyed enhanced prestige, keeping religion on the defensive. Religious beliefs were delivered a telling blow by a Pyrrhic victory in the Scopes Trial of 1925. In the words of one churchman, religion was in trouble because "those who are indentified with it, do not actually believe it."36 A sweeping charge, it was sometimes hard to refute.

Political corruption, of which there both variety and plenty in the 1920's, was an expression of the materialism and greed of the decade. The Presidency barely escaped disgrace while Harding lived and barely recovered its reputation under Coolidge and Herbert

Hoover. The great middle class enjoyed the first taste of affluent living, but suffering industrial workers employed in the sick industries of coal, textiles, and railroads, offered a sober spectacle to those who looked for social contrasts. To outward appearances, the Twenties were upbeat. Advertising combined with easy credit to bring about the great day when, in Hoover's hapless phrase, poverty would be banished from the nation. Few men had a greater impact in promoting surface level materialism in the 1920's than Bruce Barton. One of the key figures in the formation of the advertising agency of BBD&O, Barton represented Christianity as a matter of service to mankind.[39] In the age of plenty in America what better service could business perform than supplying the needs and the desires of ordinary people. Christianity had been brought to an unpredictable state by rural fundamentalists and Madison Avenue manipulators. In this litany of foibles, or in a more extended list that might be provided, it is impossible to mark any single one which did not produce a hostile reaction in Edwin Arlington Robinson. True to his artistic calling he did not often directly attack what he came to believe was the malaise of America in the 1920's, but throughout his poetry he was censorious. The decade served to identify his on-going dilemma.

Initially, at least, Robinson was most at odds with Prohibition. As someone who had done his share of drinking but who had, with the help of friends, mastered his weakness, the prospect of the government telling him that he could not have a drink was wholly repellent. He began drinking again, but only as a matter of principle. The proposition that alcohol belonged in the same category as drugs he rejected as "too silly for serious

discussion. All human beings who are not made of putty
are going to stimulate themselves in one way or another;
and alcohol, in spite of its dangers, is the least
harmful" of all the more ordinary indulgences, he
thought.38 In his balanced and sane approach to the
problem of drinking Robinson was drawing on his personal
experiences as well as his characteristic moderation.
In any event, he disliked Prohibition intensely, being
pretty well satisfied that "free verse, prohibition, and
moving pictures were a triumvirate from hell, armed with
the devil's instruction to abolish civilization...."39
The prosperity decade appeared to be otherwise to E.A.
Robinson.

More troubling than the surface events of the era,
including immigration quotas, a resurgence of the Ku
Klux Klan, the suppression of political non-conformity
and the popularity of religious fundamentalism, what did
Robinson believe were the underlying causes?   In
"Modernities," he mocked the pretensions of the day:

> Small knowledge have we that by
>   knowledge met
> May not someday be quaint as any
>   told
> In almagest or chronicle old,
> Whereat we smile because we are
>   as yet the last. --
>
> With infinite unseen enemies in
>   the way
> We have encountered the intangible
> To vanquish where our fathers, who
>   fought well,

> Scarce had assumed endurance for
>   a day;
> Yet we shall have our darkness,
>   even as they
> And there shall be another
>   tale to tell.[40]

From such gentle, indirect strictures Robinson turned to more telling commentary in his three "Demos" poems.

The "Demos" poems were an open attack on the way America moved before a democratic tide. At the same time they assist in identifying Robinson's place in the larger conflict about the future of free government in free societies taking place in American letters. Strong men had already appeared on the European horizon, for reasons traceable perhaps to either the excesses or the failures of democracy. Could America be secure against such perils? Robinson was himself unsure of the outcome for American democracy, as the "Demos" poems showed. These poems were "Demos" (1920), "Dionysus in Doubt" and "Demos and Dionysus" (1925). All three pieces revealed the poet's misgivings about democracy in action, that unless checked by some absolute moral order, democracy might conspire its own ruin by introducing a democratic slavery. The major premise of his political outlook he gave utterance to in "Demos."[41] In the poem Robinson displayed an essentially Augustinian view of human nature. The design of democracy, happiness for all, and the inclinations of individual, selfish men were contradictory because in the equality of democracy happiness was "not equal to the envy it creates." Even in a democracy there must be some to lead and some to follow so that the promise of full or total equality he dismissed as impractical and absurd.

A further expression of these abstract political attitudes was contained in "Dionysus in Doubt,"[42] Robinson's poetic protest against the Eighteenth Amendment. In this law he felt he had divined the essential danger of majority rule. He regarded Prohibition as fundamentally evil and an arbitrary invasion of the personal freedom of millions of citizens under the banner of majority rule. America might become a victim of standardized servitude which many would mistake for a highly satisfactory form of liberty. Americans were somehow convinced, he said, that in legislation they had discovered the magic wand of happiness and equality that had eluded other peoples. But to the poet's mind liberty based finally on the legislative process was not rule by the majority but tyranny by the majority and

" ... an insecure delight
For man's prolonged abode,
And the wrong thing for him to meet
    at night
On a wrong road."[43]

The danger inherent in this conception of liberty, Robinson went on to observe, was that it had no bounds, it derived its energy from legislation which of itself had no limitation. Instead, legislation was always ready for "the infliction of more liberty."[44] The result, he thought, might be a liberty which would "moronize the millions for a few."[45] In "Dionysus in Doubt" Robinson was in revolt against a middle-class tyranny that he looked upon as frightening in its effects and as all the more insidious than a totalitarian dictatorship because it was disguised as liberty.

The most trenchant statement of his doubts about democracy Robinson presented in the last of his "Demos" pieces, "Demos and Dionysus."[46] In this poem Demos was the social device that would make all men equal and happy, and thus equally happy, while Dionysus embodied man's immortal vision. The very idea of freedom Demos was seen to owe to Dionysus. Robinson again recorded the conflict which existed between equality and freedom and reproached man for having reduced everything to his own dimensions:

> ... Reason and Equality, like
>   strong Twins
> Will soon be brother giants,
>   overseeing
> Incessantly the welfare of ... all.[47]

Equality issuing solely from reason was equality uninstructed by morality. Robinson once more was disturbed and fearful that an enforced standard of equality, without regard for Dionysus, would deceive men by the appearances of liberty. Reason and equality would reduce "the obedient selves of men to poor machines."[48] In the end men would live a hive-life where art would be a "thing remembered as a toy" and the "infirmity you name love/ ... subdued to studious procreation..."[49] This denial of freedom to act -- and for men a moral freedom to choose between right and wrong, between the spirit and sin -- deleted the distinguishing characteristic of the traditional moral universe. With a sustained passion Robinson argued that the worst of all possible tyrannies could confront men in the name of

Demos,with Demos seeking to demonstrate thattradition
had made "too much of the insurgent individual."[50] The
kind of future Aldous Huxley was to foretell in Brave
New World (1932) Robinson had intimated in "Demos and
Dionysus."

Robinson's troubled mind was part of the intellectual ambiguity respecting the operation of democracy.
During the 1920's America came in for heavy attacks from
a number of literary men and women.[51] The most vehement
was perhaps H.L. Mencken, though he was not necessarily
the most perceptive. Like Robinson he struck out at the
mediocrity and conformity which democracy appeared to
demand, but his strictures were too sweeping, his
rhetoric too harsh, and his lack of an alternative too
depressing for him to be mistaken for a wise man. F.
Scott Fitzgerald was no doubt compelling when he wrote
that the 1920's saw a "new generation dedicated more
than the last to the fear of poverty and the worship of
success; grown up to find all the gods dead, all the
wars fought, all faiths in man shaken." Equally penetra-
ting was the commentary of Irving Babbitt. In Democracy
and Leadership (1924) like Robinson, Babbitt showed
himself worried about a range of problems, most of which
centered on a lack of standards for the community.[52]
Quantitatively, he realized that America had been a
great success; qualitatively, it was another matter.
Reminding his readers of Byron's definition of democracy
as an "aristocracy of blackguards," he took issue with
the Jeffersonian purpose of general happiness. Babbitt
made a distinction between equality and inverted
aristocracy, deploring the latter, and wondering
"whether in this country in particular we are not in
danger of producing in the name of democracy one of the

most trifling brands of the human species that the world
has yet seen." Whereas Babbitt was pessimistic, the
post-war John Dewey was more hopeful. In his view the
materialistic and the artistic must develop together.
He warned that the future of American society was
closely tied to the quality of education. If education
could be increasingly improved democracy would be
increasingly workable. What he found in the realities
of American education, however, raised some doubts as to
how education would infuse democracy with the necessary
social values. Too much education was in fact tech-
nical. "I can think of nothing more childishly futile,"
Dewey protested in Individualism: Old and New (1930),
"than the attempts to bring `art' and esthetic enjoyment
externally to the multitudes who work in the ugliest
surroundings ..." John Dewey wanted an educational
system which would liberate Americans from the artistic
impoverishment of a materialistic civilization.[53]

E.A. Robinson placed himself on both sides of the
raging arguments about and against America. Along with
Sinclair Lewis he deplored the small town mentality --
Sauk Center was not that much different from the
Gardiner of his youth -- and the bigotry and conformity
which described it. He readily identified with Jimmy
Herf who, in John Passos' Manhattan Transfer, refused
his uncle's offer to make him a business success. These
were dissenters of the Lost Generation which made
Robinson sympathetic with writers younger than he, if
differently motivated. Yet as an artist Robinson did
not find America a distasteful place in which to live or
to work. In 1925 The Nation conducted a writers' sym-
posium in which the question was posed: "Can an artist
exist and function freely in the United States?" For

such a question to be placed before the literary community may be taken as some measure of the seeming plight
of the artist in America. Mary Austin, the well known
writer of poetry and fiction, Sherwood Anderson, and
Theodore Dreiser all replied to the question with vigo-
rous affirmatives. None of them was unmindful of the
difficulties which the artistic temperament encountered
in a nation whose business was business. Mary Austin
saw the problem as implicit in democracy where the
notion prevails that "one person's opinion on any subject is a good as another's." "The great artist, whose
genius is in advance of his age has a bad time of it in
the United States," she admitted. Nevertheless, "there
is no country in the world today offering the artist in
any field such incomparable opportunity. The literary
artist in particular finds himself almost swamped by
fresh and exciting material, in constant flux and
speaking with vitality." Anderson and Dreiser echoed
Austin's judgments. Dreiser thought America as satisfactory and stimulating "as Russia ever was to Tolstoi
or Dostoevski, or Germany to Goethe or Schiller, or
France to Flaubert or de Maupassant ... it has all the
variations which any artist could honestly desire."
Robinson could have made much the same observations in
response to the question of the place of the artist in
America.[54]

Of the several other features of American culture
in the 1920's which the poet chose to criticize because
they were both troubling and disagreeable one or more
may be singled out. In his poems Robinson reverted to
an oblique angle of protest, casting his characters
either in remote historical times or treating the issue
by simple indirection. In "The Mill,"[55] a short piece,

his theme was the steady erosion of dignity, associated
with pride of individual workmanship, which resulted
from the growth of big business. In the poem the miller
announced simply: "There were no millers any more."
Leaving his wife in their kitchen he went to the mill
and hanged himself. He was a victim of economic forces
beyond any one man's control. The final statement of
the poem was that the miller's death would go unnoticed,
that his self-destruction, if meant as a protest, was a
futile gesture. In "Toussaint L'Ouverture,"[56] another
of the poems of the period, Robinson spoke out against
the evils of black slavery. In both "The Master" and
"John Brown" he had touched on this injustice, but in
"Toussaint L'Ouverture" he came to grips with it. Negro
slavery, in the case of the man L'Ouverture, was another
lamentable manifestation of the evils of nationalism.
Because of Napoleon's ambition for world conquest, his
personal sin in other words, society suffered and for
that reason L'Ouverture, a symbol of his race, was
enslaved. Human dignity was made the victim of

> ... a madness and a system
> And a malicious policy, all rotten
> With craft and hate.[57]

But the system was really an outgrowth of the personal
disposition of the French emperor. In the words of
L'Ouverture:

> ... I could see farther;
> And in a world far larger than
>   my island
> Could see the foul indifferent
>   poison wreaking

> Sorrow and death and useless
> indignation
> On Millions who are waiting to
> be born;
> And this because the few that have
> the word
> Are mostly the wrong few in the wrong
> places.[58]

The poet insisted that L'Ouverture, like all people of color, was a man: "God knows he was a man ... And not a piece of God's peculiar clay/ Shapen like a reptile...."[59] As the story unfolded it became clear that Robinson was attacking human greed as manifested in the enslavement of human beings. He was voicing opposition to any system in fact which aimed at leveling man to an unnatural standard.[60] And when his own nation, having cast off the formalities of slavery, looked to the star of empire for guidance Robinson was disturbed because of what it might mean in terms of slavery for the native populations encountered. Commenting on American occupation of the Philippine Islands after the Spanish-American War he had protested "the right of our incomparable republic to make a game preserve of the Philippines."[61] All this was remote from the realities of racial discrimination in the United States after World War I. A protest so indirect could miss its mark. It was a manifestation, nonetheless, of Robinson's determination, according to his artistic impulses, to question the standards of a standardized America.

Changing sexual morality, magnified by the new mores evident in the 1920's, was another of Robinson's on-going concerns as he responded to his America. As a

young man, in a letter to Harry DeForest Smith congrat-
ulating him on his impending marriage, Robinson had
remarked: "Love and lust have become so mixed up by our
poets and novelists that we poor puritans are half
inclined to wonder, as we read, whether there is such a
thing, after all, as a better motive in man and woman."
Denying that he was setting himself up for a "St.
Anthony (Comstock)," the deluge of "literary nastiness"
he judged to be a "disgrace to American letters."[62] His
third Arthurian poem, Tristram,[63] in light of such
candidly expressed attitudes,can well be taken as an
indirect protest against the sexual morality of his
times. The essence of Tristram was the love of a man and
a woman for each other and its traditionalism was rooted
largely in the poet's handling of the love theme. The
distinctiveness of the treatment of love consisted in
Robinson's clear preference for love between two human
beings as grounded ultimately on something more than
physical attraction. It must be founded in fact on
selfless motives, spiritual in some sense. Among all of
Robinson's writings Tristram was the only "best seller,"
suggestive perhaps that in the jaded 1920's people after
all were able to respond to a traditional version of
love.

     In Robinson's account Tristram had become
completely enamored of a lovely princess, Isolt of
Ireland, when he had sought her out to bring her to King
Mark of Cornwall. She was to be Mark's bride and queen.
On the night of the marriage of Mark and Isolt the lady
slipped away from the wedding feast to find Tristram.
They confessed their love for one another. Discovered
in this the King banished Tristram to Brittany where he

married another, Isolt of Brittany. She loved Tristram
but he felt only pity for her as his first love lived
on. After sometime Tristram was bidden to return to
England so that Arthur might make him a knight of the
Round Table. Meanwhile Isolt of Ireland had been
brought to Arthur's court, rescued from the cruel King
Mark. Reunited, Tristram and Isolt pledge their love
anew. Mark became conscience-stricken and permitted the
lovers to come to Cornwall where both were slain by
Andred, a benchman of the king but not acting on the
king's orders.

The traditionalism of this version of the Tristram
legend lay in the character of the love that inspired
Tristram and Isolt and the means whereby Robinson was
willing to bring it to fulfillment. Their love had a
spirituality basic to its physical expression and thus
as a grand passion it was contrasted with the marriage
of Mark and Isolt, a union devoid of spiritual rapport:
"`this offense/ To God."64 Furthermore it was a passion
which knew some bounds and would not permit a complete
renunciation of the law. Robinson had seen fit to vary
the usual renditions of epic love in three important
ways, all connoting his disillusionment with the sordid
tendencies of his day. Because of the spiritual motivation of the lovers he had not introduced the device of
the love potion in the consummation of theirlove. Not
only would the use of this artifice have made the union
unreal, it would have made it less than naturally human
and thereby less able to attain a noble expression.
Robinson attempted to add to the stature of love in
another way. Contrary to the more common versions of
the story the lovers did not consummate their love on an
immediate awareness of it. The delay described in the

poem suggested the ripening of a spiritual affinity. The physical attraction of the lovers continued ever present but it was not allowed to dominate. Finally the union of the lovers came about not as the result of decisions on their part. It was not a matter of Tristram's brute strength -- not unexpected in view of his renown as a warrior -- but of the arrangements of others.

The effect of all three of these plot variations was to underscore the nature of true love as Robinson valued it, placing him thereby squarely in a traditional frame-work. He accepted the physical side of love as natural to life as to his plot, but he preferred to emphasize other aspects of that love. Sex was no more than one element in human love and by no means the most impor-tant. The restraint and moral poise displayed in the handling of this love story was typical of Robinson's personal attitude toward man's sensual appetites and their place in literature. A moral pronounced at the end of an otherwise immoral book was scant excuse for a prolonged exposition of the sins of the flesh. Nowhere in his poetry, in fact, did he display anything but a traditional view of the role of man's lower self in the moral dilemmas of his characters.[65]

The decade of the 1920's came to an end, figura-tively at least, on Tuesday, October 29, 1929, the day the Great Bull Market collapsed, ushering in the Great Depression. The Crash and the Depression meant dif-ferent things to different people. For some it dictated the end of American finance capitalism which had been growing apace since the Civil War; to others, finish was written to the American dream as individualism gave way

to social organization; to others still the twin phenom-
ena brought an end to reckless spending and reckless
living, portending a new day if not a New Deal. Pessi-
mists were convinced the good old days were gone
forever; optimists remembered that cycles of depression
had always been followed by cycles of recovery. As for
Robinson he proposed in his last poem, King Jasper,[66]
published just after his death in 1935, that the hazards
implicit in American democracy as noted in the 1920's
had an economic counterpart in the Great Depression.
The malfunctioning of the capitalistic world, he
insisted, was in the main brought about by the same
cause that disturbed the private lives of people, a
contention between sin and the spirit.

King Jasper took its primary significance from its
symbolism of a world threatened with disaster rather
than from its story of six unhappy mortals ensnared in a
web of moral ignorance. Using characters as emblematic
Robinson enlarged on the effects of sin with a reminder
that even in an evil system it was the sins of one man,
or many men, that brought death to society. What was
important in the symbolism of the poem was not alone
what the six characters represented but the fate which
befell each of them. There was Jasper, who had built
his kingdom on the straw of his personal ambition; there
was Honoria, his wife, the sum of all that tradition
held; and there was the elder Hebron, known only in
Jasper's dream, whose initiative and genius had been
sacrificed by Jasper in winning his domain. Of the
second generation there was Jasper's son and namesake,
heir to the kingdom and wise enough to know that it was
not soundly built; there was young Hebron with his
father's genius transformed into revenge; and finally

there was Zoe, young Jasper's wife, the personification
of the human spirit, "Beauty and truth and death"
together.

It is clear from Robinson's presentation that the
sins of Jasper, greed and ambition, were fatal to his
kingdom. Jasper admitted that it was his thirst for
power that he recognized as his sin, though to an
observing world it appeared to be his lust for gold.
Yet what in Jasper's conduct merited the destruction of
his kingdom? Robinson, through Zoe, tells us that there
is a God, an Intelligence, who makes life meaningful:

> ... "No God
> No Law, no Purpose, could have
> hatched for sport
> Out of warm water and slime, a war
> for life
> That was unnecessary, and far better
> Never have been -- if man as we behold
> him
> Is all it means.67

It is precisely in the nature of Jasper's work in
raising up his kingdom that he made other men a means of
power. The roots of his kingdom went down to hell and
this was the cause of his kingdom's end. Thus young
Jasper said to the king:

> "... But a king, father.
> Whose roses have long roots that
> find their way
> To regions where the gardeners
> are devils

> May as well know there is a twilight
> coming
> When roses that were never so sweet
> before
> Will smell for what they are .... "68

As young Jasper continued, the deeper tragedy of the kingdom's decline was that the king knew enough to save his crown. He realized much better than the "red rhetoric" of young Hebron that a kingdom must be built on integrity and a virtuous regard for men, yet he refused to put himself within the boundaries of either duty or justice. At the end of the poem all were dead save Zoe, the figure of art and honesty and noble aspiration, not "bound/ Or tangled in the flimsy nets or threads/ Of Church or state."69 Thus closed Robinson's last lament for the larger tragedy of modern man.

The discernible changes which took place in Robinson's poetry over the course of the years from 1915 to 1935 were due to altered conditions at home and abroad. Historical events had taken their toll and he did not propose to disguise it. Just as the Progressive Era, and the years before, were mostly positive in their outlook for America, so Robinson, for all his private uncertainties, was prompted to look up rather than down. His move to New York City in 1899 was a sure sign of his optimism in spite of all that had befallen him. But with the coming of World War I and the resulting shocks to humanity, democracy, and capitalism he thought the prospects of his world diminished. Of the twin pillars of democracy and capitalism on which it had been built, America found these supports gravely weakened. In Robinson's view capitalism had possibly became unworkable and democracy might have developed to the point of inherent contradiction. If he continued to be optimistic, it was a more sober and a more wary attitude in light of the history of his times.[70]

IV

SOUL OR PSYCHE?

A great portion of E.A. Robinson's later work, that is, his poetry published after he had completed Merlin and Lancelot, took the form of dramatic-narratives, poems of several hundred lines or more written in blank verse. The stress placed on the inner troubles of the individual men and women in these poems caused Robinson to alternate between soul and psyche as the subject under analysis. Accordingly, he debated the ultimate nature of man. Living very close to his era he demonstrated a feel for the dilemma of contemporary humans as he proceeded to examine individuals and the circumstances shaping their lives. The age-old human failings: pride, lust, greed, spiritual complacency were all painfully apparent in his creations as at the same time the question was raised whether fault was due to maladjustment or to malice. Robinson's dramatic-narratives are a useful way to measure the mature artist. They also aid in an appreciation of the literary trends of America in the post-World War era, largely because they reveal an ambivalence in treating man's ultimate nature and final fate. There is in these poems evidence that Robinson continued to understand life as a struggle within the soul but there are also signs suggesting that the problems frequently referred to as sin arose from a conflict with the social and cultural environment. Sustained hate in "Avon's Harvest," lust in The Man Who Died Twice, selfish pride in Cavender's House, the spiritual emptiness of <u>Matthias</u> <u>At</u> <u>The</u> <u>Door</u> were all concerned with remorse of conscience which could be viewed quite as much as a psychological trauma as a spiritual experience.   In his nearness to his era Robinson achieved both a rendering of the moral problem implicit in scientific materialism and a pragmatic lesson for his fellow human beings.   But it is not always clear what he wanted his readers to believe. Remorse of conscience was a very real thing. Yet it strongly resembled a guilt-complex which could be no less real.   In any event conscience remained ill-defined beyond the step of self-examination leading on to self-knowledge. Whether it led further still, and in what direction, and with what objective Robinson did not choose to say with any greater degree of precision than most of his contemporaries.[1]

The dramatic-narratives show that despite resistance to their implications the tenets of modern thought struck hard at some of Robinson's firmest convictions regarding the spiritual side of man.   It had been against the arrogations of science that he sang some of his most mystical songs: "Credo," "The Children of the Night," "The Man Against the Sky." Yet he had not lived through an age without being affected by scientific materialism in some remarkable ways. Robinson has been called an "offspring of the scientific urge"[2] in that he seemed determined to know man and his moral problems by a consideration of the material facts as science revealed them and not by reference to an abstract theory or theories. For one thing, science precluded the finality of truth, a search for which was not long from his thoughts, but which he never dared to achieve. Once more it is evident that for Robinson the pursuit of truth belonged to man and the possession of truth was reservedfor God alone. He might be described as never having found the absolute he was searching for and which he instinctively believed did exist. In the second place, Robinson owed to the scientific temper his realism. This realism, from which he insisted he derived his optimism, was part of his keen appreciation of the stark reality of life which made up the raw material of his art. He not only wanted to face the physical, disturbing sometimes, facts but he made an intimate friendship with them an indispensable factor when he wrote. Objective reality, whether social or moral, of whatever description was for him so much matter in a laboratory. For Robinson to have imagined anything but a harshly ordered universe would not have been true to his experiences in Gardiner and New York. He was given to see the rawness of life and to detect its bleakness. Robinson was no mere recorder of facts, however, yet it is obvious that his art owed a great deal to a scientific attention to facts, the master-attitude of the age in which he lived.

In still another way the influence of contemporary thought was reflected in Robinson's work. His portrayal of character was carried out with the primitive methods of psychology, awkwardly applied. It can be argued to good effect that "what was valuable in the Freudian method was in Robinson's poetry before he had heard of Freud."[3] Freud himself made much the same general point on one occasion when he was acclaimed as "the discoverer of the unconscious." He corrected that judgment, saying that the "poets and philosophers before me discovered the unconscious. What I discovered was the scientific method by which the unconscious can be studied." It

must be added that the intellectual climate in the
United States in the post-World War years encouraged
Robinson's flirtation with the ways of psychology.
Although the artist is unlikely to be determined in his
work by the Zeitgeist, correspondingly he is unable to
avoid being touched by it. In techniques, at least,
Robinson came to owe something to psychology as he
called on the resources of the age and to which Freud
was a major supplier.

The presence of naturalism has also been noted in
Robinson's dramatic-narratives so that some of his
poetry has been called a "rebellion against being."[4] He
has been compared with Theodore Dreiser because both
sounded the "steady droning organ point of philosophical
materialism."[5] In his pessimism, which Robinson would
insist has been misread, he has been likened to Henry
Adams, finding the world a "blind atomic pilgrimage from
nothing to nothing."[6] And there is some spot evidence
of naturalism, as in "How Annandale Went Out," for
example.[7] In this poem Robinson raised the question of
mercy killing, a subject experiencing a vogue of
controversy at the time he wrote. After intensive examination of the issue and the circumstances surrounding a
particular tragedy Robinson justified the killing of
Annandale in a way wholly suggestive of the troubled
life and death of his brother, Horace Dean. In "How
Annandale Went Out" there remains, nonetheless, a note
of ambiguity, a hesitation intimated in the narrator's
lack of complete moral ease with this solution of deliberate death.

"Avon's Harvest"[8] was the title poem of a volume of
verse Robinson brought out in 1921. It was among the

first of his longer poems in which the moral purpose of
the poet was projected not in a highly symbolic form,
but told as a simple example of the reality of sin in an
average life. The sin of Avon was hatred. In his youth
he had conceived a profound revulsion in a school for a
school acquaintance. A boyhood misunderstanding had
been the occasion for Avon to strike the other boy and,
though circumstances permitted him ample opportunity for
apology, his feeling of dislike was so intense that he
was prevented from doing so. The memory of the incident
and the consciousness that he had failed his obligation
to seek forgiveness of the person he had harmed haunted
Avon for the next twenty years. On each succeeding
birthday Avon received a reminder of his attitude so
that after two decades his fear of having someday to
face his childhood schoolmate again had taken on the
proportions of an obsessive terror. The evening before
his birthday twenty years later Avon recounted this tale
to a doctor friend and revealed his fear of retribution.
So great was his remorse of conscience and his dread of
what might happen on the morning of his birthday that he
was discovered dead in his bedroom, the door locked from
the inside. In the words of the physician, "he died
because he was afraid."

"Avon's Harvest" has been called Robinson's "dime
novel" because it spoke of the horror and strangeness of
mysterious death.[9] Such a death was particularly
mysterious in the light of science and invited a psychological no less than a traditional explanation. As for
Robinson, he appeared to stress Avon's attitude as more
sinful than otherwise. Avon's fault, clearly serious,
was discussed as something not on the periphery of life
but as at its center. Avon could not escape his hatred,

try as he might. An intelligent man, he attempted to
isolate some reason for his plight. Perhaps it was
fate, "some invidious juggling of the stars;" or maybe
it was a foretaste of the eternal punishment which, Avon
believed, awaited those who could not love.[10] Even when
he was driven to think that the cause of his troubles
was not the result of free will freely exercised, Avon
spurned the idea of suicide. Agonizing over his
dilemma, Robinson allowed Avon at least a ray of hope:

> "I'm witness to the poison, but the
>   cure
> Of my complaint is not, for me, in
>   Time
> There may be doctors in eternity
> To deal with it, but they are not here
>   now."[11]

Such fleeting thoughts of eternal life should be set
against the self-analysis weakly disguised as
psychoanalysis:

> "There was a battle going on within me
> Of hate that fought remorse."[12]

The strength of these opposing forces seemed equal, with
a kind of paralysis the result. Avon was unable to save
himself and unable to look to a traditional escape by
accepting salvation. His position was basically
agnostic:

> "If such a one [God] there be. If there
>   be none
> All's well - and over. Rather vain

> expense,
> One might affirm - yet there is
> nothing lost.
> Science be praised there is nothing
> lost."[13]

Paradoxically, the science in which Avon had partly trusted was unable to account for his death. In the words of the doctor:

> "...If I were not a child
> Of science, I should say it was
> the devil.
> I don't believe it was another
> woman.
> And surely it was not another man.[14]

Such a passage revealed a very narrow definition of "science," one confined to the bio-chemical side of life. The modern psychologist would be in a much better position to understand and appreciate the possibility of fear-induced death. "Avon's Harvest," that odd combination of the old and the new, was consistent with a changing America. The misadventures of Avon remained sin in the old-fashioned sense of the word, of that there is no doubt. As there was no salvation in the poem, mere explanation sufficed, an explanation which betrayed a psychological answer.

No single poem in the group of dramatic-narratives gives a completely final answer to the question of soul or psyche. Much of the fascination of these poems, in fact, arises from the shadings and variations which feature Robinson's outlook quite as much as, in their

peculiar way, they suggest the uncertain response of his
America to the same question. The Man Who Died Twice[15]
is without doubt the poet's nearest approach in his
longer poems, if not in the whole of his work, to a
traditional religious experience. Fernando Nash was a
wretched sinner who succeeded where Avon failed because
he came to terms with God. Nash's victory can be
ascribed directly to God and the part God played in his
life. In the poem God was a personal being, offended by
man's actions, and divine justice had to be satisfied by
a complete dedication of the sinner to God. As seen
from another perspective, however, a Freudian interpretation of the breakdown and recovery of Fernando Nash is
also plausible: the ego gradually working itself to a
level of expression from the id, and then through the
functioning of moral conscience and self-criticism
developing toward a state of contentment associated with
the super-ego. No doubt Robinson's reliance on the
language of salvation is sufficiently persuasive to
encourage the conclusion that The Man Who Died Twice
told a religious experience, but with some justification
Nash's personality, it can be said, was that of a
patient relieved of anxiety and guilt through auto-
suggestion.

The story of the fall and rise of Fernando Nash was a
simple and direct one. A man of near great musical
artistry, Nash had wasted his talents by debauchery:
sins of pride and of the flesh were committed with a
degrading regularity. The subliminal character of such
behavior is hard to ignore. In time Nash became just
another piece of nameless refuse who had cast off his
human dignity, "God's too fallible image."[16] Only the
grace of God rescued him from the usual fate of such

unfortunates. Thus inspired, he came to realize the evident worthlessness of a soul divorced from God. As a penance for his sins and as praise for God in rescuing him from a spiritual death Nash rededicated his musical genius, not to composing music, but in beating a drum for a group of street-singing evangelists. Once more Nash is seen as sublimating his desire, though in an unexpected and highly unconventional fashion.

The sins of Fernando Nash had a dual character. Because God singled him out from the average with a gift of rare talent he turned to sin when he failed to become recognized for his genius. The source of his downfall was pride. Before his moral eclipse he was inordinately proud of his musical talent. His conscious need for praise swelled an innate selfishness. That his desire for popular acclaim did not keep pace with his accomplishment drove him to forsake his demon for the devil. The sins of the flesh, the devil, and devil-women, lusts and drunkenness were his escape, as well as balm for his wounded pride. The sorry result was described in the words of Nash himself:

> "... look at Fernando Nash
> The heir-apparent of a throne
>   that's ashes,
> The king who lost his crown
>   before he had it,
> And saw it melt in hell.[17]

As Robinson probed a psyche, he discovered a soul. The sins of Nash were much more than his revenge for not having achieved worldly recognition for his music. The enormity of his misdeeds lay, rather, in his disobedi-

ence to God's law as the realization of this engulfed
him. Robinson left no doubt that Nash was crushed by
remorse because he had been given to see that his pride
was an offense to God. It was this awareness, as it
burned into his consciousness and his conscience, that
prompted him to estimate himself a "bloated greasy
cinder," "a crapulous and overgrown sick lump/ Of
failure and premeditated ruin." Exploring Nash's condition, Robinson went on to have an old friend of Nash
describe perceptively the feelings of someone without
spiritual anchors. Such a soul was in

> ... the Valley of the Shadows -
> A region where so many become so few
> To know, that each man there believing
>   himself
> In his peculiar darkness more alone
> Than any other.[18]

Here Robinson had taken hold of the traditional state of
a soul in sin: the supernatural companionship that it
longed for, however it might be sublimated in this life,
was denied, and that by a free act of the will. The
resonances of the orthodox theory of sin and redemption
were unexpectedly faithful for a poet writing in an age
of rising material expectations, though no doubt many
Americans who read The Man Who Died Twice found nothing
novel or psychological in Robinson's account.

The despair which this realization engendered in
Nash would seem to be an almost ideal situation for the
kind of suicidal reaction which can be found elsewhere
in Robinson's poetry. The "escape" of suicide did enter
into the thoughts of the dejected composer, only to give

way to the central idea of the poem, Nash's return to
God. His night of the soul issued into a spiritual
catharsis, altogether traditional in its scope and
meaning, when his sins were pardoned by the same God
they had offended. How else explain the constancy of
purpose of this drum-beater for the Lord? For Fernando
Nash his salvation was an "inviolable distinction,"[19]
yet Robinson, in the words of his character, knew that
this seeking after God was in no way unique. As Nash
told his friend:

> "... I shall not annoy you
> Or your misguided pity with my
>   evangel,
> For you must have yours in
>   another dress.[20]

Robinson was saying, in short, that all men must in
their own way seek God, though wisely he did not insist
that everyone must suffer the extreme degradation and
crushing remorse of the tragic composer, Fernando Nash.
It is possible that Robinson's special sympathy for his
own creation, Nash, may have derived from the popular
coolness with which his early poetry had been greeted.
As for Nash's sins, they are another reminder of the
mighty fact of conscience in the American psyche, no
less than in the poetry of E.A. Robinson.

In Cavender's House,[21] another of the dramatic-
narratives, Robinson again concerned himself with sin,
but with sin considered also as a crime. To add to the
timeliness of the story as well as to make it more
macabre the setting was the business world and the
matter around which the action revolved was murder. In

the poem Cavender, upon his return to his finely appointed mansion after a long period of absence, was confronted by the visionary figure of his wife, Laramie, whom he had slain twelve years before. Laramie was only a projection of Cavender's conscience for he had killed her in a fit of jealous rage. He had suspected her of being unfaithful to him and since the commitment of the crime he had been haunted by the uncertainty of Laramie's infidelity. This was the question he asked repeatedly of Laramie on the night of his vision of her. Since she was only the product of his overwrought conscience, or imagination, no answer to his question was forthcoming. Cavender's agony of remorse was climaxed when he was made to realize by his conscience that not Laramie's infidelity, but the selfish pride that motivated his suspicion, was at the root of his spiritual unrest. The strength to face himself and his punishment in the hope of a future reward, which amounted to a restoration of his sense of integrity, was his salvation in the poem.

Robinson's appeal to both the moral and the civil law, given the actual and the pending changes in American jurisprudence at the time, is something of a dissent from trends in American law. Consistently concerned with the moral implications of human behavior in Cavender's House, he also made an appeal to civil law, thereby inferring that the civil law ought to take into account in its rulings the internal character of human actions. For Robinson internal motivation was more relevant than the external effects of behavior and for that reason should not be ignored by civil judges. He was, in this respect, taking issue directly, if indeliberately, with the school of legal realism which had

gained great prominence in American jurisprudence by the
1920's.   In the nineteenth century legal theorists both
in Great Britain and the United States had advanced the
proposition that the law does not and should not propose
to judge human behavior as God might judge it, from the
inside out.   The Courts, instead, should base decisions
on an assessment of the social consequences of human
actions.   Such an assertion was part of the larger
argument against absolutes in the law, part of the
nineteenth-century intellectual revolution against all
absolutes whatsoever.   This position gained a wide
number of adherents among lawyers and judges, especially
after the turn of the century.   Modes of American legal
thought were, in fact, drastically altered.   Applica-
tions of this rule of social consequences might have an
unquestionable benefit, as in the passage of benign
social legislation based on sociological findings; or
questionable results as in cases where citizens were
denied rights because, when exercised, there might
follow what was estimated to be a bad effect on society.

At the time when Robinson was busy writing his
dramatic-narratives no legal theorist offered a more
outspoken or insistent defense of legal realism than
Jerome N. Frank.   Frank was a practicing attorney, a
lecturer at the Yale Law School, and he would be one day
a judge of the United States Circuit Court of Appeals in
New York.   In his book, Law and the Modern Mind
(1930),23 Frank made a strong case for his view that law
must be treated as a social and not a moral phenomenon.
One of his assumptions was that people were decisively
affected by their environment and therefore it was their
environment which made them saint or sinner.   One of his
corollaries was that an improved environment would pro-

mote obedience to the law. In any event, men and women as individuals were much less accountable for what they did in Frank's judgment than was maintained by the traditional view of crime. Many criminals, Frank further contended, were driven to lawlessness by an inner subconscious revolt against the authority of their father, the father-image. In opposing the law they were relating to it as a father-substitute. Law thus conceived was an absolute. While such an approach to law might be useful in a primitive society, thought Frank, in a mature and civilized state it was no longer relevant. The law could not be used as a series of prohibitions on the assumption that some actions were intrinsically bad. It must be used instead as a means of accommodating change. As Frank summed up his argument: "the stage of complete maturity is reached when the relativity of all truths is accepted."[24] This was a moral/legal world little to the liking of Robinson.

Not taking direct exception to the school of legal realism and perhaps but generally aware of it, Robinson's world of crime remained a matter of justice related to motivation. Cavender had taken a life,and the natural law via its adjunct, the civil law, required confession and punishment. But this was also the nature of the moral law in the objective determinates of sin. If an act was evil it should be punished because of the character of the deed. For Robinson the moral law and the civil law were the same in substance and in method. However, even before the civil law could bring sanctions to bear, Cavender's conscience had punished him. The remorse of his conscience stemmed both from the nature of the deed and from the bad effect it had produced on another person. That Robinson did not call up the

obvious sanctions of hell-fire is to miss the more
subtle and, in view of his wariness about theology, the
more real aspect of sanctions for him. It should not be
overlooked that the vital problem was not Laramie's
unfaithfulness, if such there had been, but rather the
admission by Cavender that he had sinned against pride.
The crime of Cavender was one which began with pride and
from which issued murder. Murder was punishable at law
and the civil law would have its day. But if justice
meant anything to Robinson the deep-down motivation must
also be punished.

The crux of the poem was Cavender's belief in God
and thus the moral sanction of reward and punishment.
Unless he had some such belief his twelve years of
mental anguish were inexplicable, given the sentiments
expressed in the poem. At two distinct points Robinson
spoke of Cavender's belief in God, examples suggesting
that as the poet conceived Cavender's moral problem,
faith in God was essential to the salvation of the hero.
In the first instance Cavender outlined the necessity of
the existence of God:

> "... Is there a God?"
> He asked. "Is there a Purpose,
>   or a Law?
> I thought there was; or I should
>   not have suffered
> So cruelly more for you than for
>   myself."[25]

It was this conviction which deterred Cavender from
suicide. Later he remarked that there must be a God,
"`or if not God,/ A purpose or a law.'" Otherwise,

Cavender continued, the world was surely a seeming endless incident/ Of doom ....'"[26] At once he knew that if he thought this, then suicide would come easily. It was equally plain, however, from Cavender's outlook, that although God certainly existed any attempt to define the concept, whether anthropomorphic or otherwise, was not important. Unlike Fernando Nash, Cavender did not pray to God for strength and Laramie rebuked him for this failure at the outset of his vision of her. Nonetheless Robinson was clearly more taken with an ethical system which had historical roots in theology than with theology itself. This is what he had in mind in sounding a censorious note on the general spiritual apathy of the age, where people's faith

> "... when they are driven to think
>   of it
> Is mostly doubts and fears....[27]

Cavender's House was a convincing example of Robinson's deep concern with the spiritual flux of the America of which he wrote and from which he had himself sprung.

Given the fact of fast-changing America in the 1920's, was anyone really listening to what the poets, Robinson among them, were saying? Were the poets talking to themselves rather than to a wider audience? The best-selling Tristram (1927) provided some evidence that Robinson was being read, while poets like Conrad Aiken and Archibald MacLeish were gaining reputations as critics and spokesmen for contemporary morals and mores. During the decade Greenwich Village took on the veneer of radical chic with Edna St. Vincent Millay among the most prominent of the new Bohemians. She won a Pulitzer

Prize in 1928 for The Harp Weaver and captured much of
the spirit of the era in her oft-quoted line: "My candle
burns at both ends." There was little that was obscure
in Stephen Vincent Benet's John Brown's Body despite its
symbolism, whereas Robinson Jeffers in Tamar and Other
Poems (1924) and Roan Stallion (1925) betrayed a sense
of decay that seemed incongruous in an America enjoying
both peace and prosperity. Nonetheless there is justification for raising the question of the extent of the
reading public when it came to poetry and Robinson made
one or more contributions to the poetry of the remote,
if not the obscure.[28]

The obscurity of modern poetry, as with much of
modern art whatever its form, was widely acknowledged in
America in these years. Inspired by the psychology of
Freud and Jung a new language with a new vocabulary were
needed to satisfy the impulses of the unconscious.
Words took on strange meanings which the poet alone
might intend them to have, language as communication
changing to stylized self-expression. The general
public had to work out its own set of criteria for the
acceptance of every contemporary art form. In the case
of music it was melody; for poetry it was clarity.
Another way to express clarity, which had especial
reference to the Twenties, was "ease." The Prosperity
Decade had virtually exploded with new gadgets, motors,
and machines to make life easy. It was easier to drive
to work than to take a train, it was easier to flick a
switch for washing clothes than to scrub them by hand,
it was easier to go to the movies than to read a book.
Poetry was no exception to this ever-expanding rule that
life in America was to become easier. A poem which was
not clear was not easily understood and thus not likely

to be read. Ezra Pound, T.S. Eliot, E.E. Cummings all suffered much the same fate with the general public because they failed to pass the clarity test so that more and more, poets talked only to each other if not to themselves alone.

E.A. Robinson shared in this general neglect to a goodly extent, tarred with the prevailing idea that modern poetry was not very intelligible. Curiously enough he was suspect not because he had created his own language. His readers knew what his words meant; they were not so sure of his traditional morality. His concentration on sin and human frailty, resulting in pangs of conscience, struck many as simply too old-fashioned. He continued to fight the old battles of good versus evil drawing on the spirit of Jonathan Edwards, however much his poetry might be streaked with Freudian implications or agnostic doubts. It was for this reason that Robinson seemed out of place quite as much as other poets who were modern in outlook but frustratingly obscure. Such a consideration mad Robinson's personal dilemma as an artist -- reminding his countrymen of the values inherited from the past whatever the allure of the present -- a better barometer of the American mood and outlook than the artistic adventurings of the more avant-garde literary figures. Calvin Coolidge was an updated Puritan -- to Walter Lippmann he was Puritanism deluxe -- and America liked Coolidge as well as bath tub gin, Babe Ruth, and the "talkies." The country continued to believe in sin, if a little less so in damnation, but at the same time it wanted to do as it pleased. The two tendencies, theo-retically at odds, were nevertheless features of the decade. Not that there was any room in Robinson's poetry for playboys. To him life remained ever the serious endeavor. Going on a binge was after all a popular rendering of self-indulgence and with such human weaknesses Robinson could not compromise his moral principles. The Glory of the Nightingales was a case in point.[29]

The protagonist of this poem, Nightingale, was cast in the mold of a successful materialist who made his own rules for living and who did not much care who was hurt in the process. His unscrupulous conduct had enabled him to ruin his physician-friend, Malory, in a business venture. As a result Agatha, Malory's wife, whom Nightingale had wanted for himself, died and Malory became a wanderer. The physician returned some years later, determined to kill Nightingale for his past deeds, only to discover the intended victim a physical wreck. Nightingale, amidst the splendor of his wealth and possessions, was near death. Just as the years had built up within Malory a distorted idea of retribution, so Nightingale, his life about to end, was full of remorse. He confessed his failures to Malory and sought to make some personal amends to him by providing in his will for the endowment of a hospital. Having made a material compensation for his past, Nightingale then committed suicide.

This brief sketch of The Glory of the Nightingales readily suggests the observation that the spiritual salvation which Robinson had proclaimed in The Man Who Died Twice and Cavender's House is strikingly absent; but it also hints that for some at any rate material compensation may be all of which they are capable. Drawn as Robinson might have been to the traditional versions

of salvation he was enough a child of his time not to
insist on single answers. In place of the faith of
Fernando Nash or the resignation of Cavender the con-
fines of Nightingale's world were clearly marked by
suicide, which stood as a re-assertion of his materialism. By taking his own life he had insisted on the
right to continue to make the rules of living and the
final rule of dying. The salvation in the poem remained
a material achievement, a kind of remorse and satisfaction which Robinson is not prepared to dismiss as either
unworthy or unhuman. Nightingale may have been meant to
represent the familiar figure of the tycoon turned
philanthropist, seeking to reimburse society for his
social sins with the means of overcoming certain worldly
ills, his new hospital.

American philanthropy in large measure had grown out
of the gifts of self-made men who had been ruthless in
their determination to succeed, men like Nightingale.30
Lacking an aristocracy in the Old World sense and
priding itself on the possibilities of self-improvement
through self-help, America waited upon the success of
the Gilded Age before it displayed the munificence for
which it has become noted. Robinson grew up a product
of that Age and came to understand that business success
usually involved a devotion to "making money" that in
past ages had been reserved for the worship of God. The
"diabolical dirty race after dollars" had soured the
young Robinson, yet not to the point of condemning all
business men in his poetry. In The Glory of the Nightingales the poet is mostly the observer, showing the
spectacle of selfishness producing ruin and death and
yet, somehow, seeking to redeem itself in a wholly
earthly manner. It is manifestly difficult to general-

ize about the motivations of the American business leader as philanthropist. Daniel Drew in his business endeavors has been described as a "master fleecer of lambs," but he founded Drew Theological Seminary. Andrew Carnegie had a deeply personal commitment to provide opportunities for average citizens to use the twenty-five hundred libraries he endowed -- the "universities of the people" -- which combined equally with his passion to promote international peace. Not only did he give away nine-tenths of his three-hundred million-dollar fortune, he affirmed the doctrine that surplus wealth was a sacred trust. In The Gospel of Wealth (1900) he wrote that it was the "duty of the man of wealth to set an example of modest, unostentatious living, shunning display and extravagance, to provide moderately for all wants of those dependent upon him and, after doing so, to consider the revenues which had come to him simply as trust funds." Not every American philanthropistwas so articulate, much less so well disposed. But a great many of them, brought up in Christian and humanitarian families, made conscious efforts to do good. Sometimes the fortunes were so immense that that factor alone required the establishment of a foundation. The Rockefeller Foundation which was set up in 1913 was especially generous in gifts for medical research. Money from the foundation helped to control or stamp out hook worm, yellow fever, and malaria and gave direct aid to medical schools. Indeed, in keeping with the dream and reality of American life, most benefactors directed their gifts to medical and educational enterprises, though museums and art galleries benefited greatly as well. John D. Rockefeller, like Daniel Drew, was something of an exception in his proposal to make the University of

Chicago a great Baptist institution, though church-
related schools and hospitals benefited the churches
indirectly through the contributions they received.
Robinson's use of philanthropy appeared to make amends
for individual past actions of questionable morality;
this was natural enough in the socio-moral climate of
the era and one which would be believable. The Glory of
the Nightingales in this respect possessed a timely
social dimension.

In the poem Robinson suggested a direct relationship
between evil and remorse. Nightingale was presented as
a materialist who was part of a larger materialist
universe. His was the story

> Of a worm boring in a noble tree
> And one there was no need of saying
>   over:
> Nature had made the tree had made
>   the worm,
> And Nightingale was not responsible.[31]

Consistent with Robinson's vision of things there had
occurred in Nightingale's youth a struggle between good
and evil:

> "... I had enough of other vision
> To see the other side of selfishness,
> But I had not the will to sacrifice
> My vanity for my wits ...."[32]

Somewhat strangely, given the denouement, much was made
over the role of the devil in the troubles of Nightingale, an attitude hardly in keeping with the naturalism

of contemporary literature nor consistent with the poem itself. But Malory, the injured party, rebuked Nightingale for blaming the devil for his faults:

> "But why the devil do you insist so
>   hard
> On devilish help in your duplicity?"
> Malory asked, and scowled at
>   Nightingale.
> "You know your work and what was
>   coming of it
> Or might come ...."33

After a while Nightingale was moved to admit that "The devil is only part of destiny." The impression persists, nonetheless, that these figures, Malory and Nightingale, were inhabitants of a post-Christian culture. The central Christian concept of love was impractical and Nightingale, the materialist, did not pretend to understand it. Love formed no part of his attraction to Agatha, for example; the Christian life was one which none could live. What remained was a kind of "natural justice," well exemplified in the lines assigned to Malory as he gazed upon the disease-ridden body of Nightingale:

> A tired bacteriologist, seeing
>   him there
> Might say there was a God. Nature
>   at least
> Had never done her work so well before
> Or saved a man of science so much
>   trouble.34

This reference to a natural order of justice is reenforced by the view that Nightingale's consciousness of
wrong-doing was mostly a psychological awareness and not
remorse of conscience. As his wrongdoings had left ill
effects which were to him material, so he compensated
for them by his material gift of a hospital to provide
for the sick of body.

Robinson's ongoing mood, a gloomy one as he confessed
in one letter to a friend, was especially pronounced in
Matthias at the Door.25 The poet's mood, in turn, could
have been a direct reflection of America in the depths
of the Depression, Matthias at the Door having been
published in 1931. These were grim days and Robinson
had written a grim poem replete with destruction and
self-destruction centering around three suicides, with
only an occasional ray of hope growing out of self-
analysis. The Great Depression was the most serious
shock suffered by American society since the Civil War.
Poets perhaps only somewhat less than stockbrokers were
affected by the phenomenon of a prosperous and proud
nation suddenly and totally plunged into the economic
mire. Robinson was not intent on providing his own
reasoned assessment of the Depression in Matthias at the
Door. That would come in King Jasper. But the per-
vading sense of ruin, given so strong an emphasis in
Matthias at the Door, was completely consistent with the
country's fallen state, just as the hopes of Matthias
for the future based on a simple refusal to embrace
suicide was akin to the nation's conclusion that it had
no choice but to plod on.

At the same time, Robinson satirized the American
success story, the stereotype of which he had beenat

odds with for most of his artistic life. Matthias was a wealthy man of conventional faith. The suicide of Garth, a family friend, was the occasion for learning that his wife, Natalie, had married him out of gratitude. Really in love with Timberlake, she married Matthias because he had saved Timberlake's life. The old love of Natalie and Timberlake was rekindled when by accident they met at the scene of Garth's death. They were discovered by Matthias who put the worst possible interpretation on their meeting. Thereafter Natalie continued to be Matthias's wife until in a fit of depression she took her own life. Timberlake too committed suicide but not before insisting that Matthias must seek a new meaning to his life. The lives of Garth, Natalie, and Timberlake have been unnaturally subordinated to the needs of Matthias's conscience. The sins of the latter were those which Robinson was wont to ascribe to the business materialist: he was a practitioner of commercial wiles, often at the expense of others. Matthias was described as a "rich web of complacency,"[36] his only thoughts on the meaning of life the "common fears" of growing old. He paid lip service to the divine, yet hung on to his beliefs, such as they were, because he had nothing else to fall back on:

> ... "If my faith went out,"
> He said, "my days to be would all
> be night--
> A night without a dawn and no lamp."[37]

Yet when his wife committed suicide the faith of Matthias was completely shattered. It had served a pragmatic function, supplying a supposititious purpose for life. Being artificial it collapsed in the crisis created by Natalie's self-destruction. Typically Robinson had woven a pattern of inter-personal relations which demanded some kind of resolution, and no less characteristically he pointed in the direction of some kind of extra-personal phenomenon. For example, Timberlake advised Matthias to believe in something supranatural:

> "... Hold fast, Matthias.
> There is not a man who breathes and
>   believes nothing.
> So you are done with mysteries. If
>   you are,
> You are the one elected and fulfilled
> Initiate and emeritus of us all."[38]

But Robinson offered no more than a mystery, the nature of which was hardly implied. The message was, in fact, a negative one. Wealth and science did not have the answer to Matthias's dilemma; the "`chips of brief experience,'"[39] which were all mankind had, could offer nothing positive or delineated. If the three suicides of the poem are taken literally Matthias at the Door is a grisly and melancholy tale, and comes as something of a reminder that Robinson was by no means free of the obscurity of language and meaning associated with more avant-garde poets. The dark underside of life as portrayed here, furthermore, tends to redefine Robinson's pessimism as sometimes uncompromisingly bleak.

As in Tristram so in Talifer 40 (1933) Robinson chose to explore the nature and place of marriage, but this time in a contemporary setting. What he asserted about marriage would be sure to reveal something of his thought respecting man's ultimate nature: soul or psyche. Despite a celibate life he showed once again that he retained a strong interest in human love and its conjugal expression. His traditional outlook was pronounced. Whether he was reacting sternly against the increasing laxity of American mores in this respect, or whether he was simply setting forth his views, the result was much the same. The evidence remains clear if fragmentary that Robinson judged physical union without love as lacking a critical element, a judgment which was part of the story of Talifer.

Talifer was the portrait of a man searching for a "temporal absolute," termed peace, through the most intimate of human relations, marriage. The story was told of Talifer, a man of wealth and background, who for unaccountable reasons suddenly decided to marry Karen, a coldly intellectual woman of surpassing beauty, rather than the warmly human Althea he had courted for some time. The marriage with Karen proved ill-advised, however, and Talifer was especially miserable. Karen solved his difficulty by leaving him, convinced that Talifer intended her physical harm. She fled to Wales with Dr. Quick, a friend of Talifer. But there she found her retreat a boring trial. Karen soon left Quick for Oxford and the intellectual life she longed for. Quick returned to Talifer two years afterward to discover that his old friend had married Althea. The soap opera of a later day could hardly have a more routine story line.

It was in Dr. Quick's commentary on the marital mistakes of Talifer that the poet spoke. While Talifer exhibited a certain morality regarding the sanctity of marriage, even though it was conceived in passion, he was happily rid of Karen in exchange for Althea. Dr. Quick made some predictable observations concerning Talifer's actions and their place in the scheme of life. For one thing, Quick maintained that the marriage of Talifer and Karen was joined by God. He also told Karen that her reason for marrying Talifer was simply the desire to have what Althea wanted, a sick motive for a divinely sanctioned union. Her pride completed Talifer's lust as the cause of the unhappiness of the marriage. The rising American divorce rate notwithstanding, Robinson's view of marriage was rooted firmly in the past. <u>Talifer</u>, as a poem, has been called trivial, a bad poem even, so that it is difficult to see more in it than a passing reavowal of the need for a higher motive in marriage. Perhaps only that larger social purpose, well removed from the obvious intention of the author, allows it a place in Robinson's ongoing role as social critic.

If a good many poets of the time were writing in languages all their own, Robinson, in his dramatic-narrative, <u>Amaranth</u>,41 appeared lost in his own peculiar world of thoughts. The whole of the poem has a ghostly, not quite real cast; the characters inhabit a nether world familiar to Robinson alone, a shadow place full of men who have not heeded their "inner light." The protagonist of the poem, Fargo, a painter turned pump-maker, was given to see that making pumps could be a sublime achievement, if to do so was God's will. The poem took its title from the being ... spirit ... shade, Amaranth, who guided Fargo through the shadow realm. To look into the eyes of Amaranth was to see yourself for what you were. Amaranth was, in other words, a figure of conscience and his role in the poem pointed unerringly back to Robinson's obsession with self-knowledge as a first step toward whatever salvation might be possible. The several characters whom Fargo met on his journeying were satirically portrayed. A clergyman, Pascal Flax, had only "`the lost assurance of right and wrong/ Of True and false....'"42 Figg became a lawyer because it was the thing to do. The poet, Pink, refused to honor the wisdom of the age, wanting to plant without roots. One special reflection ascribed to Pink was that God exists with certainty, but that men cannot know him while they are among the living, an adumbration, perhaps, of Robinson's own view of the divine. Indeed, Amaranth included a number of large themes discernible in the total of Robinson's work: philosophical idealism, scientism, and of course tradit-ionalism. But the poem was couched in language and evoked a mood so peculiar to the individual artist that the dilemma Robinson perennially faced respecting the primacy of values in his poetry was accordingly obscured.

The dramatic-narratives, taken as a group, are perhaps the most likely place to discover Robinson's idea of man. Created by the mature artist, they are rich in musings on the troubled destiny of the human breed. Devoid of symbolism, the single life or lives in the poems are studied with an intensity which emphasizes the value of the individual. Placed in what appears to be mostly twentieth-century settings, they exhibit atti-tudes of fear and hope harmonious with the era. In response to the question: soul or psyche? a composite answer emerges. The common elements are salvation gained through self-knowledge. The salvation is spiritual, even supernatural at times, or it is material, but it is there. Furthermore it is salvation of the individual which is stressed consistently, a consideration which tends to underline this basic preoccupation in Robinson and his America. The self-knowledge is either remorse of conscience or psychological awareness, though the former appears to be Robinson's real preference. The faults which self-knowledge reveals are invariably sins as historically defined and understood, theologically inspired in the remote past but now transmuted by science into something else. Yet for Robinson the mystery of man and his ultimate purpose remains. He had not gotten much beyond the wisdom of the ancients and, equally significant, had not discarded that wisdom for what science taught. Theologians and philosophers had posited the mystery. Poets and all creative artists had been better able to persuade people of the presence of mystery in their lives.

Where did Robinson stand in relation to literary-social critics of the 1920's? By insisting on the mystery of man's being, he cut across the grain of strictures being laid down by commentators like Harold Sterns and Joseph Wood Krutch. In his essay, "The Intellectual Life," Sterns explained that recent American intellectual life had been feminized largely because of the pioneer spirit of the American male who allowed women to toy with ideas as men did the work of building the nation.[43] Even so, went his argument, women were interested in the intellectual life as a sociological activity, the application of ideas to produce solutions, the outcome of which had been predetermined. There had been in America of late no real regard for intellectual activity or values as such.

E.A. Robinson should be exempted from the judgments of
Sterns, however. While admittedly concerned with man in
society he offered no instrument of reform or improvement, dwelling instead on the first principle, man's
nature. Robinson was an intellectual as well as a poet,
his sensitivity and moral insight as manly as the early
Puritans whom Sterns so much admired.

Joseph Wood Krutch in "The Modern Temper" wrote a
particularly influential analysis of the 1920's, finding
in the period an end to spiritual comfort for mankind.[44]
For Krutch humanism was dead and it had been slain by
science. "With increasing completeness," he wrote,
"science maps out the patterns of nature, but the latter
has no relation to the pattern of human needs and
feelings." He summed up his outlook with one crisply
stated conclusion: "What man knows is everywhere at war
with what he wants," a judgment offered with the confi-
dence of the philosopher-king "armed with the certitudes
of science." In such criticism Krutch was in good
intellectual company, thinkers like Bertrand Russell and
the American historian Carl Becker. In The Heavenly
City of the Eighteenth Century Philosophers (1932)[45]
Becker took occasion to write: "Edit and interpret the
conclusions of modern science as tenderly as we like, it
is still quite impossible for us to regard man as the
child of God for whom the earth was created as a
temporary habitation. Rather must we regard him as
little more than a chance deposit on the surface of the
world, carelessly thrown up between two ice ages by the
same forces that rust iron and ripen corn...." Robinson
refused to accept this merciless explanation and
rejected the proposition that the past was dead. His
poetry derived so much of its strength from the mystery

in the universe, and the values of the past added so much meaning that without these sources his work would have lacked force and direction. If Edwin Arlington Robinson "was the most profound of the twentieth century American poets," as Henry Steel Commager insisted at mid-point in the century,[46] he was atypical of the modern temper, rejecting its scientific dogmatism -- while showing it a proper respect -- in favor of a more uncertain and therefore a more human vision.

Under pressure brought to bear by the threatened triumph of the philosophy of nihilism, so well represented in the totalitarian fascisms and communism of World War II and after, Becker choose to embrace the value-oriented society which he and others had helped to undermine. In New Liberties For Old (1941)[47] Becker praised the values associated with teachers from Confucius to Jesus which "readily lend themselves to rational justification yet need no justification." Is there not discernible in this reversal a recognition of the humanism of Robinson? Large questions pertaining to him nonetheless remain. Was his outlook so atypical of the modern temper and was his insistence on the mystery in life so a scientific as to reduce him to the status of an interesting anomaly or raise him to the condition of a prophet? Can the artist ever expect to escape the quandary in which his art places him? Does the lesson of the myth of Sisyphus become a necessary element in the dilemma of the artist? Such questions may seem to carry with them their own answers, and not the least so for E.A. Robinson.

In other words, Robinson does not appear to be without real doubt concerning man: soul or psyche. His avowal of the mystery of life is at once too personal and too indefinite to be persuasive of others. Robinson's misgivings can be related directly to his idea of God. A preference for soul over psyche points to the God of the Scriptures or a variation thereof rather than to a Force or a Purpose in nature. Had he chosen to stress reason rather than soul, some kind of construct of a Supreme Intelligence would have been feasible. But he did not, opening the way to a more drastic repudiation of the old religion and the old God by others willing to take the step from which he, the misplaced Puritan, refrained.

V

AN IDEA OF GOD

It is evident that Robinson's poetry was preoccupied with the question of good and evil, and with the relationship of man to God as this might explain the moral troubles common to mankind. His poetry also displayed an ongoing response to his America. As the nation and its people changed, were confronted with new issues as a result of new experiences, or as it was assailed by fresh doubts about its present and future mission, so Robinson attempted to chart it all. From beginning to end his work responded to the rhythms of America. In this process, from beginning to end, he wrestled with an idea of God. Throughout his lifetime, and therefore across the broad expanse of his literary output, an idea of God was never far from his concern; to seek to discover and to possess a satisfying idea of the Divine was a habit natural to his mind and to his spirit. Not that it ever threatened to become his exclusive occupation; Robinson was too much a child of his age which was scientific, empirical, materialistic, skeptical. But an idea of God nevertheless overarched the entirety of his life as a poet. Assessing the nature of that idea is to argue in favor of its critical importance in order to gain a fuller appreciation of the dilemma of Robinson as an artist and of the dilemma of his America as well. Like the American people Robinson was derived from a religious state of mind. History had broken that mold, yet the materials might still be reworked into some meaningful and satisfying semblance of the old God.

In every civilized age the ultimate challenge has been to come to an understanding of the meaning of life. Man's place in the universe was a predictable theme in Robinson's poetry. Almost invariably this search for meaning has led to speculation on the existence and nature of God. Even in those philosophies in which God is denied, the fact of denial tends to occupy a significant place in the system of thought proposed to account for man without God. Neither Robinson nor his era could claim exemption from this historic mandate. Robinson's idea of God represented a natural progression from his idea of man. His concern for God consistently broke through the surface of his poetry, whatever the immediate subject or purpose might be.

In the popular mind God and formal religion are closely linked. Not so in Robinson's poetic vision. A reviewer of his first published verse, The Torrent and the Night Before, had charged him with representing the world as a prison house. The poet protested that while the world was not a prison, it was "a kind of kindergarten where millions of bewildered infants are trying to spell God with the wrong blocks." Many years later, when asked about this remark, he excused himself by admitting : "I was young then and it was a smart thing to say."[1] Together these two statements suggest that from the first it seemed right to him that people should try to spell God's name and fathom the meaning of the divine. The lamentable aspect of it was the "wrong blocks." The suspicion arises immediately that some of the wrong blocks Robinson associated with the churches. His youthful outburst against Trinity Church, Boston, and all it signified to him, has already been recorded. As for his personal commitment to the creed which produced the churches, he confided to Arthur Gledhill in 1896: "I fear I haven't the stamina to be a Christian -- accepting Christ as either human or divine."2 Christianity and the churches were so thoroughly identified with one another that the rejection of the latter made retention of the former a dubious proposition. For Robinson, as for many of his generation, to leave the church was to leave behind Christianity as well. Yet to read "A Christmas Sonnet For One In Doubt,"3 published in 1925, is to realize that the problem of God was ever fresh in his reflections.

Robinson's desire to stand apart from the churches was maintained to the end of his life. He was quite explicit on the point in a letter to Laura Richards, written in 1933. "Leaving out the Romans and the Methodists, there does not seem to be much left of the churches but the buildings. Even the Romans will have to contrive some sort of symbolic compromise before long; and as for the Methodists, who come nearer to ruling us than we suspect, they are perhaps more an incorporated and shrewdly organized ignorance than they are a church, and the Church of England is more like a social club, with music and trimmings, than like anything in the Scriptures." So much for the churches. As for theology, Robinson was equally negative. "The Christian theology," he went on, "has so thoroughly crumbled that I do not think of any non-Roman acquaintance to whom it means anything - and I doubt if you do. The Christian ethics might have done some good if they

had ever been tried, but I'm afraid it's too late now."
As for the future, the poet was no less dogmatic.
"There's a non-theological religion on the way, probably
to be revealed by science when science comes definitely
to the jumping off place. It is really there now, but
isn't quite ready to say so."4 This latter aspect of
his outlook he developed further in another letter to
Laura Richards, written about the same time. "As for
religion of the future," he predicted, "I didn't say
that it wouldn't be mystical. Of course it must be that
in order to be a religion, but it will be free of all
theological machinery. I suppose you know about the
recusant gentleman who said he might believe in the
Trinity when he saw one man riding in three carriages."5
The tone and substance of such remarks make it plain
that Robinson's idea of God had little or nothing of
formal religion about it.

Because the distinctive religion of Robinson's
America was Protestantism it was against that form of
Christianity that his criticism must be measured. In
ways America by the 1920's had entered into a post-
Christian era; it might also be described as having
moved into a post-Protestant phase. America from the
days of the first settlements was a Protestant country.
Then came the flood of Catholic and Jewish immigrants in
the late decades of the nineteenth century and thence
down to 1914, challenging Protestant hegemony. But it
was not simply a matter of numbers. The adjustments
involved theology as well as social changes, none of
which was easy for the Protestants to manage. Protestantism had grown complacent about its superiority,
having been so long in an accustomed position of domin-
ance. The very successes which it enjoyed in the

earlier times tended to make the Protestant community
smug and intolerant. In any event Protestantism relaxed
at the very time when it ought to have girded itself to
meet new challenges. The clear field so long enjoyed
had brought about an erosion in its theology. As there
had been no need to maintain a strong theological structure, no such structure was maintained. Furthermore,
the appeal to the heart, which was typical of Protestant
denominations in general, was consistent with romanti-
cism which went hand in hand with revivalism. Limited
stress was placed on doctrinal definitions or serious
Scriptural study. Theology as an intellectual discipline, noteworthy for rigorous thought or training, was
neglected. The Protestant minister was first of all,
and generally speaking little else than, a preacher of
the Word who sought to bring men and women to God by
appealing to emotions. For the intellectual classes
before the Civil War a de-Christianized religion,
Unitarianism, orTranscendentalism took up some ofthe
slack, but in ways hardly beneficial to orthodox
Protestant theology.6

In early America Protestant Christianity had been a
powerful formative force. The work of Jonathan Edwards
was theological first of all, from which came recurring
waves of the Great Awakening. But the process which
commenced with a culture being molded by religion, by
the close of the nineteenth century, had become a
religion molded by a national culture. To be truly
American was to be Protestant as well, in the eyes of
those who had long held the reins of power. America was
the cutting edge of the Protestant advance, so well
illustrated by the intention of the American Protestant
Missionary groups to "Christianize" the Filipinos after

four hundred years of Spanish presence in the Philippine
Islands.

With their intellectual defense in disarray Protestant
leadership was vulnerable to the demand that religion
conform to changing cultural values as well as to the
aggressive flow of the American experience. Americanism had literally swallowed Protestantism. The new
scientific hypotheses posed problems for Scriptural
interpretation; psychology provided a substitute for
conscience; Christian charity easily turned to the
humanitarian concern of philanthropy. A religion that
had long been fed by the non-theological springs of
Evangelicalism was ill-prepared to maintain the old
order of things and on many counts failed to do so. At
least the evidence to this effect was substantial enough
to have given Robinson and others reasons for declaring
that Christian theology, in the poet's own phrase, had
"thoroughly crumbled." There is no way of telling how
Robinson would have responded to the Protestant theological revival of the 1940's under the lead of Reinhold
Niebuhr and Paul Tillich, particularly given Niebuhr's
rejection of human perfectability and his renewed stress
on sin. But Robinson's antipathy to the churches seems
too firmly entrenched to have been touched significantly. Besides it was Robinson's experiences as an
artist in his own life time and his response to the
problem of God that mark the boundaries of his part in
the dilemma of the artist in America, and to which his
attitude toward the churches offered some intimation.

Robinson's suspicion of the churches was ingrained,
emotional, and highly personal. He did not think
historic Christianity represented the pure teachings of

Jesus. In his view St. Paul had changed these teachings by introducing an ascetical element which had not been present from the beginning. When pressed on one occasion to be explicit about what teachings of Christ Paul had modified Robinson was unable to be definite. Perhaps a professor at Harvard had said as much, or possibly it was an attitude traceable to some German book of higher criticism pored over years before which caused Robinson to differentiate Christ from the primitive church.[7] All of this was a puzzle to certain of his friends who were church-goers. In spite of his suspicions of the churches he was to acknowledge on one occasion that he believed himself very close to institutional Christian faith. Theodore Maynard has recounted the incident as the outgrowth of a conversation with Robinson in which Robinson brought up the topic of religion. Their talk concluded with Robinson saying: "Well, Maynard, though I suppose you and I would use a somewhat different terminology about such matters, I think at bottom we hold much the same beliefs."[8] As Robinson knew Maynard to be a sincere church-goer, such a remark cannot be dismissed as altogether off-handed. It revealed to some degree a sympathy for what the churches taught, if not for the churches as institutions.

While many of Robinson's poems spoke of the problem of God in a materialistic society, one in particular dramatized his dilemma over the place and function of the church, "Ponce de Leon."[9] The story of Ponce de Leon as Robinson depicted it was in keeping with his conviction that sooner or later a man must look to his inner self as the first step in atoning for his misdeeds. The sins of Ponce de Leon had been social as well as personal

because in giving way to his ambition evil followed for
many people. Critically wounded in his search for the
fountain of youth, in the poem he has retired to Havana
to die. As he awaited the end of life his despair of
God's mercy turned to hope. Certainly the moral problem
here was one common to the dramatic-narratives, but with
a difference. For historical accuracy and intelligibil-
ity Ponce de Leon, as a Catholic, was in need of a
Catholic's consolation in overcoming his state of
despair. To speak this consolation was a sage-
physician, though in one of the early drafts of the poem
Robinson had made the sage a priest rather than a
doctor. The change occurred despite objections raised
by friends, protesting that the only important thing for
a Catholic at death would be the chance for de Leon to
confess his sins to a priest.[10] Non-sacramental words
of comfort would not be enough. Unable to bring himself
to this solution, very possibly because of his skepticism toward institutionalized religious practices,
Robinson chose to make the sage a physician. In the
poem as it finally appeared the resolution of the
problem remained somewhat ambiguous, as the sage-
physician said:

> "when you have revealed your
>   memories
> To your confessor, and have made
>   your peace
> With God you will be wiser, and
>   be done
> With fear, which I see written
>   on you still.
> Your pain will then be less your
>   enemy

Than fear is now."11

The element of confession was present. But it appeared not as part of the action in the poem. Reference was confined to an allusion, a technique which implied the poet's hesitation about the efficacy of confession as a sacrament dispensed by an institutional clergyman.

In "Nicodemus"12 Robinson took up the theme of the competing and conflicting demands of a living faith and an institutionalized belief. Nicodemus, a man attracted to Christ as a healer and more than a healer, was a Jewish nobleman, a member of the Establishment. He saw at once that following Christ brought him into opposition with the established order of things, both in terms of church and state. The poem was made up of an extended conversation between Nicodemus and Caiaphas, the latter representing a strict adherence to law and custom. Robinson expressed Caiaphas' attitude in a number of sharply worded descriptions.

> "Our laws and Caesar's are enough,
>   God knows,
> To keep the safest of us occupied
> With not forgetting them."13

> "The laws that were our fathers'
>   laws are right
> For me."14

> "There is a covenant that has not
>   changed
> And can not change."15

> "... the old laws
> Unfailing and unchanged and firm
>   as ever."16

These and like passages were used to place Caiaphus in
direct contrast to the burgeoning faith of Nicodemus in
a "mad man" called Christ. The conclusion of the poem
strongly implied that Nicodemus remained unshaken in his
faith. The overall impression of "Nicodemus", however,
was that of the mind-set of Caiaphus, symbol of institutional religion, against the tortured faith of Nicodemus
which fell outside the bounds of the law. While the
poet's sympathies doubtlessly lay with Nicodemus,
Caiaphus was made to appear as smug and certain of the
law and perhaps the more memorable character.

For most nineteenth-century American Protestants the
Bible was an important part of education as well as a
source of faith and a standard of conduct.[17] Robinson
was part of that tradition, though he repudiated the
faith commitment involved. Like the average American of
his time for him the Bible and its stories, characters,
and lessons, its language and resonances were things to
be appreciated as appropriate to great literature.
Robinson wrote any number of Biblical poems, including
"The Three Taverns," "Lazarus," and "The Prodigal Son."
In other poems wide use was made of the Scriptures by
direct extraction or passing reference so that,
considering the total body of his work, the impression
is strong that Robinson was familiar with the Testa-
ments. From Genesis alone upward of thirty references
can be identified; he drew heavily on the Gospel
according to Matthew; and, as in "The Three Taverns,"
made much of the work of St. Paul as the Apostle to the

Gentiles. All this might amount to no more than outward
signs, evidence which in itself suggests that the Scriptures influenced Robinson largely at the cultural level.
The salient question is whether or not the Bible
message, the "good news" of the Gospels, for example,
played much of a role in his outlook, and if so, what
inferences were there which pointed to his idea of God.
Robinson did not reflect the simple promise of Redemption, but he did make use of the "mystery of rebirth,"
itself a central consideration in the New Testament.
Rebirth is a general proposition, however, logically
related to the Scriptures but not exclusive to
Christianity. In this respect the influence of Christianity might well have mingled with similar sentiments
discoverable in Eastern religions of which Robinson was
knowledgeable. But in his strictly Biblical poems, with
their obvious source in Scripture, the mystery of
rebirth appeared genuinely Christian in inspiration,
without amounting to a confession of faith on the part
of the poet. The mystery of rebirth, with the implication of the need to become again as a child, merged with
one of the main currents of literary thought from
Hawthorne and Melville through Henry James to William
Faulkner. Robinson was both carrying on and enriching
this important literary strain.

The teachings of the Scriptures Robinson accepted as a
rare wisdom. By no means a close student of the Bible
he was at home with it in a way which reemphasizes the
Bible's place in American culture and American religion.
Approaching the Bible with genuine reverence he proposed
to use it with respect both as to accuracy and inspiration. But did this reliance on the Bible tell anything
concrete about his idea of God? Robinson chose his

Biblical materials carefully and in so doing presented a God who was a kind and loving being. Most of all Robinson's God expected men to choose the spiritual over the material by a conscious conversion, and thus there was no place for a predestining deity in his thought. One had to make a decision to be saved, a reaffirmation of the nineteenth-century Protestant celebration of the heart over the head in the salvation process. Looking at Robinson's Biblical idea of God from a negative perspective, his poems did not represent God as vindictive, as bent on dispensing justice or eager to cast offenders into the everlasting fire. Such an idea of God had no place either in Robinson's poetry or in his life.

General impressions notwithstanding, the poets of Robinson's time used Biblical settings on occasions. William Vaughan Moody's "The Death of Eve" and Robinson Jeffers' "Dear Judas" are good examples. Perhaps of Robinson it must be said only that he invoked the Bible more frequently than did others, a fact which may have derived from his own personal search for faith. His Biblical poems, done mostly in the 1920's, represented an interest in religion not generally associated with Robinson or the decade. Indeed, these poems hold a noteworthy place in the literary history of the period, testimony that despite the pretensions of science and the appeal of materialism Americans still liked their Bible and their God.

Robinson's negative evaluation of the Christian churches and their theology and his frequent use of Biblical materials are suggestive of his idea of God. But the proposition invites a direct and studied consideration to obtain a fuller understanding. In a real sense Robinson had a problem with God, to a large extent the problem of God in a modern society where traditionalism remained vital to the way of life of countless of its members. Focusing on the idea of God, or Divine Force, in the work of a poet-intellectual like Robinson provides a better awareness of the total worth of his verse. It helps to locate him more precisely in the growth of American literature. Finally, it rounds out his dilemma as an artist.

Robinson's approach to God in his poetry was, perhaps, as illuminating as any aspect of his total artistic expression. His attraction to the God of his fathers and the ethical values that inhered in the ancient religion was inimical to his philosophical awareness and the instruction of science. The endurance of a traditional religious concept of God and the appeals of philosophical and scientific assertions about the probability and the probable nature of some Divine Force created a tension in both the poet and his work. Without this conflict Robinson would be considerably less interesting as an artist and also less important as an intellectual whose keenness to enjoy both the assurances of the scientific world and the reassurances of the world of faith was an instructive detail in the larger canvas of American thought.

Three major themes were at work on Robinson, affecting his vision of the Divine, each of them intrinsic to the American mind. The Self of Idealism, the "no-God" of science, and the Father of traditional Christianity were all discernible in various passages of his poetry, explaining Robinson's reluctance to be very

specific about the nature of his deity. His penchant
for philosophical Idealism has been to an extent
discussed. Two of his best poems, "The Children of the
Night" and "The Man Against The Sky," contained noteworthy evidences of his fondness for an Idealistic
interpretation of the universe. Letters to friends
leave little doubt that Robinson went through an Idealistic phase; the phase passed or weakened while its
effects on his idea of God remained. The consequences
of his contact with Royce and others were especially
relevant to his reluctance to be definite about the
nature and quality of the divine, just as those same
influences worked to insist on the actuality of some
Divine Force. Knowing well the argument that the
taproot of the subconscious went down to God, the one
Self called the Absolute, he was not entirely convinced.
He followed the line of the argument without adopting
its conclusions, reserving the privilege to interpret
the existence and function of God as accumulating
thought and experience might suggest.

Robinson's enthusiasm for Idealism was stubbornly
subdued by science, much as he sometimes appeared subdued by life itself. His peculiar optimism and his
verging agnosticism were born as much of personal defeat
as they were products of a world scientifically
measured. Yet this infiltration of science had impact
after all. The tenets of science undermined much of his
Idealistic and religious conceptions of God. They also
encouraged in Robinson's poetry a recourse to scientific
methodology which scorned first principles in favor of
what the specific details might yield by way of understanding why man must accept his lot, "to grin and bear
it." The realism of his verse he owed to the scientific

temper so that God in either the traditional or philo-
sophic sense was alien corn not likely to ripen into
full fruit. In such poems as "Lost Anchors" life became
meaningless and futile. As late as 1934 Robinson found
himself writing to Laura Richards:

> I'm afraid, on the whole, that isn't
> much comfort in nature as a visible
> evidence of God's infinite love. It
> [the world] appears to me to be a
> shambles and a torture-chamber from
> the insects up -- or should we say
> down? The insects will have the
> world some day, and maybe they will
> eat everything that's on it, and
> then eat each other. For some
> reason or other this makes me think
> of an epitaph by Thomas Hardy. You
> may know it?
>> "Im Smith of Stoke. Aged sixty-odd
>> I lived without a dame
>> From youth time on; and would to God
>> My dad had done the same."[18]

In such moods even the stern God of his Puritan fore-
bears enjoyed no place because the poet found too little
meaning to life itself.

Robinson was a Puritan, whether or not he was a
Christian, and the marks of it are everywhere in his
poetry. Preoccupation with the themes of sin, conscience, and self-knowledge often led to some of his
best verse. In "Siege Perilous"[19] the poet-moralist
warned that men must not be seduced by the easy way of

materialism, even though the world was replete with good
men confronted by misfortune and men of indifferent
virtue prospering as the world prospers. Instead a man
must trust his conscience and his God. If he did this
he could ignore the rest of men:

> There fell one day upon his eyes
> a light
> Ethereal, and he heard no more men
> speaking.

The power of conscience was the very marrow of the old
New England theology and Robinson sang such songs of an
inner necessity. His commitment did not include a
willingness or a need to define God metaphysically or to
discuss the Heavenly City. It addressed itself instead
to man in his moral relationships: with God and his
fellow men. Attimes Robinson displayed an essentially
religious version of men, and by inference, of God,
espousing a kind of tendential Christian theology.

A degree of caution is in order in characterizing
Robinson's adherence to a traditional view of God, for
the very reason that he declined to be specific about
the subject. In his poetry God was not so much a person
as a force, a Divine Force for Good, which motivated men
and turned them in the direction of the Ultimate. Was
he not, perhaps, articulating his own version of Alfred
North Whitehead's concept of God as interdependent with
the world and developing with it, at a time when Whitehead's effort to formulate a system of universal ideas
was much talked of? In any event, for Robinson man's
vision was not an awareness of the majesty of the God of
Moses, but the need of man to know himself and thereby

to attain a meaning beyond himself. This was the Divine
Force for Good that Robinson discovered and so often
revealed in the tangled lives of his characters. His
reluctance to personalize God was attributable both to
Idealism, which tended to reduce the moral force in the
universe to a point where a single word or sound, Self
or the Absolute or "ooom" sufficed to identify the
deity, and to the sway of scientific agnosticism in
which God was unknown and perhaps did not exist at all.
Occasionally Robinson's verse seemed to personalize God,
but more often his deity remained "the great What-ever-
it-is."

The interplay of the Self of Idealism and the God of
tradition, with lingering doubts about the existence of
a deity, when examined in some detail, spells out
Robinson's appreciation of the Divine Force for Good in
human experience. His shorter verse, his "songs with
souls," presented an initial way of understanding this.
Robinson retained an affinity for short verse throughout
his career so that this particular form encompassed the
full range of his thought. So far it is clear that
uncertainty about the "eternal verities" stalked him at
almost every turn:

> We know not, dying what we may be,
> dead,[20]
> We know not, living, what we are,
> alive.

These lines, written in 1890, aptly pronounced
intellectual indecision. But it was an uncertainty that
drove Robinson to sing of the need of belief and to
delineate men who were seeking fulfillment. To assess

further the Divine Force for Good it becomes necessary
to turn again to three major poems, "The Children of the
Night," "The Man Against The Sky," and "Captain Craig."
These are poems of great density and of high yield, so
that by focusing on the elements of the divine in them
Robinson's idea of God becomes more intelligible,
typifying both faith and doubt. "The Children of the
Night" was a simple confession of faith in God under-
taken by the poet as an individual who was sure of man's
essential dignity and his eternal destiny. It was a
destiny culminating in God, the Light as spoken of in
the poem. To Robinson Light and the Divine were
synonymous. The initial use of the figure of Light is
instructive in that it suggests the presence of both
Idealistic and Christian versions of the Divine mingled,
unself-consciously, in a single poem. In one place
Light was identified with Self.

> So let us in ourselves revere
> The Self that is the Universe![21]

Yet Robinson did not remain satisfied with the extent of
this assertion. He was drawn irresistibly to the God of
his fathers. In sensing this he allowed for the traditional God, from his own lonely station as a man and on
the premises that men have used with respect to God:

> If there be nothing, good or bad,
>   But chaos for a soul to trust,-
> God counts it for a soul gone mad,
>   And if God be God, He is just,
> And if God be God, He is love.[22]

The apparent traditionalism of this profession should
not obscure the fact that the poem proposed to endorse
no finalized way of judging God's nature, relying
instead on the "common creed of common sense." In "The
Children of the Night" Robinson took occasion to flay
formal religious confessions of God:

> we have played enough
> With creeds that make a fiend of Him.[23]

This passage suggests not alone the influence of
Idealism but antagonisms bred by the failures of
formalized religion and the pretensions of the higher
criticism as well. "The Children of the Night" may well
be called "the breakdown of the old belief and the
endeavor to find life without it,"[24] but enough of the
traditional God remained to render the poem a fine
example of the interplay of the conflicting ideas
seeking to dominate Robinson's version of God.

The tension arising from this interchange served, at
times, to face Robinson in the direction of agnosticism,
as, for example, in "The Man Against The Sky."[25] In
this poem was represented the whole human race in one
man, a modern Everyman, in whom were cast the doubts,
the fears, the aspirations of twentieth-century
scientific man. The hero of the poem was real in that
these feelings and convictions had been part of his
earthly labor. In one man he was all men,

> As if he were the last god,
> going home
> Unto his last desire.[26]

Throughout Robinson demonstrated the human thirst for
some kind of reassurance from philosophy, yet it was a
philosophy and not a religion which was espoused. God
became the Word, the Self, ill-defined if not undefined.
In one way "The Man Against The Sky" portrayed the
struggle within Robinson between the old Christian
faith, which science had made increasingly difficult for
him to embrace, and the Self of the philosophers. At
times he hovered between the two attracting forces, as
when he wrote:

> The Word itself, the living word
> That none alive has ever heard
> Or ever spelt.

But, unlike a formal Christian, Robinson could not make
a further appeal to Revelation in order to attain a
fuller awareness of God. For him in "The Man Against
The Sky" the certainty of the Word was enough. Apart
from this unwillingness to define the Word Robinson had
restated and in some ways appeared to advance a
religious belief. He was quick to affirm human dignity.
Why did men continue to live and to propagate, if the
world of nature was in fact but a

> ...screeching lewd victorious derision
> Of man's immortal vision.[28]

Man was no mere mechanism assigned some unfathomable
role by some unfathomable force and thereafter consigned
to extinction. Man was more than matter. Based on his
experience with people Robinson was led to think of God,
to infer God. But the only tangible aspect of God was
the operation of an ethical system amongst men, the

Divine Force for Good in everyday lives.

The poem, "Captain Craig," stands out as an affecting limning of this concept of a Divine Force for Good. Doubtful that he could know very much about God directly or theologically, Robinson was equally sure that he could recognize the divine elements in his fellow human beings. In "Captain Craig" he set forth his idealized view of man, revealing how this Divine Force ought to assert itself in human affairs. The philosophy of "Captain Craig" [29] implied that above the brotherhood of man Robinson was drawn to a Fatherhood of God. Craig was heard to avow the existence of God and he told something of his nature. God was inscrutable but he was all-just and all-loving.

> "There is no luck,
> No fate, no fortune for us, but the old
> Unanswering and inviolable price
> Gets paid: God sells himself eternally,
> But never gives a crust." [30]

This appeared to be the same God as found in "The Children of the Night," whose make-up Robinson there chose to define as justice and love. God "sells" himself in his love for mankind, but men must be disposed to love God in return. This is presented as part of God's justice. He never gives even so much as a crust unless men are willing to receive Him.

"Captain Craig" also contained a statement concerning the passage of man to God. The more obvious means was love for human beings, yet in the poem Robinson asserted that charity was best based on faith,

a mystic supra-rational belief. This faith should not
be conceived in fear, furthermore, but in a complete and
utter trust in God, a

> "wise kind of joy that you shall have
> Never, until you learn to laugh with
> God."31

Robinson probed the phenomenon of faith. He showed it
to be a simple trust in God and a desire to carry out
His will. Such a faith was a gift not always given.

> "It is the flesh
> That ails us, for the spirit knows no
> qualm,
> No failure, no down-falling: so climb
> high"32

God was reached not "alone through flesh contempt/ Or
through flesh reverence." This ascent to God was made
easier by a firmness of faith. The stronger the faith,
the more certain the salvation, a conviction movingly
analogized in Craig's dream of his encounter with the
Carpenter from Nazareth. Clearly Robinson appeared at
home with the God of tradition in these passages. Yet
it is well to remember that what he had to say about God
was inspired not by the deity of Idealism or the God of
the Scriptures, but by his realization of the Divine
Force for Good in men's lives. It was from the human
situation that the poet implied a personal God that was
quite traditional at times, it was not from some a
priori notion of the divine. This may be the same as
saying that he admired the Christian ethic while
resisting the accompanying concept of God. But it was

the old God that we discover him in the process of resisting, and in some ways none too successfully. The Divine Force for Good was the everyday experience of God for E.A. Robinson.

Other of the poet's "songs with souls" tell of the conflicting elements in his approach to the divine. In "Credo"[33] he wrote:

> For through it all-- above beyond
> it all--
> I know the far-sent message of the
> years
> I feel the coming glory of the Light.

In such verse the inscription of Idealism was convincing. Yet consider, in contrast, the fervent message, the agonized faith of "Calvary,"[34] with its final question:

> Tell me, O Lord -- tell me, O Lord,
> how long
> Are we to keep Christ writhing on
> the cross!

If taken out of context of his total poetry "Calvary" appeals to us as a poem worthy of one who confessed the Father in the Son. It is fair to suggest with respect to the kind of God Robinson believed in that there were times when he could only accept "the Self that was the universe" and that at other times nothing else would satisfy him than a belief in "The Master who toiled along to Calvary." Neither the Idealistic vein nor the Christian mood dominated, however; neither was as

consistent as Robinson's acknowledgement of the deity as
a Divine Force for Good.

The Arthurian trilogy and the dramatic-narratives
affirmed a moral foundation to life but they were
notable as well for a hesitancy to avow an absolute God
or immortality. Roman Bartholow[35] was one of the first
of the narratives exploring the spiritual state of the
time and reiterating the lessons of Lancelot, that man
of his nature seeks a spiritual goal. The sense of sin
symbolized in Merlin also figured prominently. Simply
told, Roman Bartholow was the story of modern man's
saturation with materialism and his attempts to overcome
this condition. The poem revealed in an important way
Robinson's grasp of the values in that it narrated the
personal triumph of a morally sick man. Bartholow faced
a spiritual impasse:

> Like one above a dungeon where for
>   years
> Body and soul have fought futility
> In vain for their deliverance.[36]

He was able to find himself and rise above his weakness
because he came to a belief in God. The figuration
assigned to the deity,

> Power
> That filled him as a light fills a
>   buried room
> When earth is lifted and the sun
>   comes in,[37]

delimited knowledge of the nature of the divine. Yet in gratitude for his deliverance through faith Bartholow invoked God, hinting at some form of a personal deity. Roman Bartholow had three important ingredients which were consistent in Robinson's religious verse: a sense of sin or failure, a need to believe in Something, outside of man, and a passage to God on the strength of faith. But the poet hesitated to personalize the deity, save by faint implication, preserving his preference for a Divine Force for Good as the essence of his awareness of God and man together. The absence of a Divine Force for Good in the lives of the people as in The Glory of the Nightingales enables us to appreciate the humanistic morality Robinson at times so much favored, a reminder of Robinson's ongoing uncertainty about God. The absence of God in the poem does not suggest at all that the human resolution utilized to demonstrate salvation or healing had any less meaning for the people involved because God was not directly part of the drama. To Robinson human or worldly redemption could be satisfying.

What conclusions may be drawn about Robinson's idea of God? A consistent awareness of man's frailty and his struggle against that condition in order to achieve some kind of self-mastery and self-fulfillment are the starting points for recognizing Robinson's acceptance of a divinity. Usually for him human fulfillment is explained by reference to the Divine Force for Good in the lives of men. There is some power and purpose that form part of the universe, accounting for man's desire for self-satisfaction of a high moral order and imparting to him the stamina to achieve his special dignity. At this level of definition Robinson's belief

in a deity is not open to question. Beyond this
definition, however, conflicts must arise about how far
he went in the direction of defining God. Perhaps some
useful distinction can be made between Robinson's
traditional well-limned God, and his ill-defined deity
of Idealism and the scientific temper, by distinguishing
between what Robinson wanted in God and what he was able
to accept intellectually. That he wanted (and in ways,
needed) the God of Revelation seems practically certain.
That is why he wrote, subconsciously perhaps, as though
there was such a deity and his belief in him was quite
real. But the positive thrust of philosophical Idealism
and the negative effects of scientific thought prevented
him from enjoying the anthropomorphic consolations that
belief in a personal God held out. His heart and his
mind were at war. Nor did the fully mature artist move
finally in one direction or the other. All three major
sources of his idea of God he continued to draw on
throughout his total verse; the passing years witnessed
a retention of an indefinite idea of God. Like his own
generation of Americans, Robinson in his poetry revealed
a need for God, whether out of historic habit or something deeper which had given rise to that habit. Yet he
remained puzzled as to God's knowability according to
any but a worldly form.

AFTERWORD

The art of Edwin Arlington Robinson mirrored both
the sources of the American mind of his generation and
the growth nurtured by these sources. By the time of
his death in 1935 the stamina of the ancient ethical
code, attenuated to be sure but powerful still, was as
evident as the maturation of scientific thought.
Americans as a nation continually sought a composition
of these divergent systems simply by acting as though
there was no fundamental conflict between the two.
Their action thus taken proceeded on the basic pragmatic
supposition that if a workability between the two could
be discovered and demonstrated, then the truth of the
compatibility of faith and science was certified. In
considerable measure the effort succeeded as new principles from life were adopted at one end and old ones,
not yet absorbed or sloughed off, were retained at the
other. For Robinson personally his thought attained no
such resolution. His failure cannot be lightly dismissed as the resulting paralysis of excessive reflection,
however. It should serve, instead, as an annotation of
the persistent uneasiness in American culture about its
ultimate purpose. The unresolved conflict within his
art between what tradition held and science taught is
evidence that Robinson had some disturbing doubts about
the collective myth of the American historical experience, the multi-faceted jewel of the "American mission."
Both in theory and in fact, in his undisguised contempt
for the imperialists of 1898 and in his reservations
concerning the nature and functioning of democracy

Robinson had come to have doubts about the national
destiny, even as he clung to the dignity of mankind.
His own judgments amounted to little, perhaps, because
he was no mover or shaker. But his misgivings were
symptomatic of a growing disenchantment of many American
artists and intellectuals with the old order, including
national greatness and purpose. This is a strange and
unexpected conclusion about a man who was genuinely
traditional if not conservative. Robinson discerned
what many Americans were reluctant to admit, that
America was becoming progressively less unique among
nations, its reputation as the world's last best hope
surely dimmed. In the transition of American thought
the erosion of the sense of mission which had depended
intrinsically on the old verities provided the conditions proper to the life of an intellectual radicalism
which Robinson's thought helped to adumbrate. His
deeply felt attachment to the past, his poetic temperament, the particular years of his life span all worked
to confine his contribution to this radicalism to that
of allusion rather than definition. Increasing numbers
of American artists and intellectuals, however, would
take the step the poet for his part was unable and
unwilling to: a considered rejection of the collective
myth. As for Robinson, in the realm of his own art, he
stood face to face with an innate human desire for
salvation, nirvana, fulfillment, and the scientific
postulates of a purely bio-chemical humanity. Too
firmly rooted in the past to renounce the old morality
which called for the old God, too much a part of the
present to discount the scientific doubts cast upon his
mind, he left a legacy of anxious qualm as to the
validity of the pragmatic solution. The American temper
in the fifty years since Robinson's death has continued

to display this disquiet, only partially obscured by the apparent success of faith and science yoked together for the common good as determined by a current majority.

NOTES
FOREWORD

[1]Edwin Arlington Robinson, Collected Poems of Edwin Arlington Robinson (New York, 1948), p. 1201. (Hereafter cited as Collected Poems).

2Archibald MacLeish has given some notice to Robinson as an authentic American voice in "On Rereading Robinson, Appreciation of Edwin Arlington Robinson, Richard Cary, editor (Waterville, Maine, 1969), pp. 3-5; p. 4. Yvor Winters, "Religious and Social Ideas in the Didactic Work of E.A. Robinson," Arizona Quarterly, I, Spring, 1945, reprinted in Appreciation of Edwin Arlington Robinson, pp. 134-146, asserts, somewhat tentatively, the social side of some of Robinson's poems. Chard Powers Smith, Where The Light Falls A Portrait of Edwin Arlington Robinson (New York, 1965) discusses Robinson's poetry as art, pp. 334-344, as does W.R. Robinson in "The World as an Aesthetic Phenomenon," Edwin Arlington Robinson: A Poetry of the Act (Cleveland, O., 1967), pp. 118-133.

3Robinson wrote in this vein to Richard Watson Gilder. "The predominance of this willingness to be honest, with never a suggestion of surrender -- or even of weariness -- is to my mind the most admirable thing in life or in art -- provided always that the artist has the faculty of being interesting." Robinson to Gilder, Dec. 22, 1908, Selected Letters of Edwin Arlington Robinson, Ridgley Torrence, editor (New York, 1940), p. 65. (Hereafter cited as Selected Letters).

NOTES
CHAPTER I

[1]Hermann Hagedorn, Edwin Arlington Robinson (New York, 1938) takes steps toward treating Robinson as part of his times, largely because of the stress of his human qualities.

[2]Of a number of general commentaries which give more than passing attention to Robinson, Henry Steele Commager, The American Mind (New Haven, 1950), pp. 156-158 is both perceptive and stimulating while Van Wyck Brooks in New England Indian Summer, 1865-1915 (New York, 1940), pp. 491-500, is less imaginative and less positive.

[3]For an historian's summary of how Robinson saw the Gilded Age see Charles A. and Mary R. Beard, The Rise of American Civilization (New York, 1930), pp. 383-479. By their analysis of the Gilded Age the Beards make it easy to identify Robinson's sympathies with whatever Progressivism he became aware of during the era of Theodore Roosevelt.

[4]"I have to acknowledge that New England is in my blood and will not be denied." Robinson to Laura E. Richards, Aug. 10, 1923, Selected Letters, p. 134.

[5]Robinson to Lewis M. Isaacs, July 9, 1923, ibid, p. 133.

[6]Collected Poems, p. 415.

[7]John A. Kouwenhover, Made in America The Arts in Modern Civilization (New York, 1948) helps to identify the dilemma of the artist in America. Henry F. May, The End of American Innocence (Chicago, 1964) weaves the problem into the main theme of his study.

[8]Robinson to Harry deForest Smith, Sept. 27, 1890, Untriangulated Stars, Letters of Edwin Arlington Robinson to Harry deForest Smith, 1890-1915, Denham Sutcliffe, editor (Cambridge, Mass, 1947), p. 4. (Hereafter cited as Untriangulated Stars).

[9]Robinson to Mrs. Louis V. Ledoux, Aug. 14, 1916, Selected Letters, p. 98.

[10]This New England connection is worth a word. For example, though Oliver Wendell Holmes, Jr. and Robinson never met, the Justice did read some of his poetry. Morris R. Cohen was the common friend; he sent Holmes a volume of Robinson's poems in 1927. Holmes's reply was characteristic: "Robinson has a poetic gift and his words leave an echo -- but it seems to me the echo of an echo. His music on the mystery of life does not quite enchant me -- and I suspect, though this should be said with trembling, that he is a little too serious about man for an ultimate." Nonetheless Holmes was not wholly unmoved and promised Cohen he would "read more." Holmes to Cohen, Sept. 21, 1927, "The Holmes-Cohen Correspondence," Felix Cohen, editor, Journal of the History of Ideas, Vol. IX, 1, Jan., 1948, pp. 3-56; p. 46.

[11]Hoyt C. Franchere, Edwin Arlington Robinson (New York, 1968), p. 15. Smith, op. cit., p. 70.

[12]Robinson to Smith, Jan. 13, 1893, Untriangulated Stars, p. 80.

[13]Robinson's relationship to his family is probed with great sensitivity by Smith, op. cit.

[14]Quoted in Hagedorn, op. cit., p. 286.

[15]This evaluation of Mary Robinson follows Smith, op. cit., pp. 69-73, who goes well beyond Hagedorn in detail and speculation. For a different estimate of Mary Robinson see Louis Coxe, Edwin Arlington Robinson The Life of Poetry (New York, 1969), p. 31.

[16]The influence of Swan and Schumann are highlighted in Hagedorn, op. cit., pp. 25-37. For a further account of Schumann's role see Peter Dechert, "He Shouts to See Them Scamper So: E.A. Robinson and the French Forms," Appreciation of Edwin Arlington Robinson, pp. 335-345.

[17]Leo Marx, Machine in the Garden (New York, 1964) develops themes relevant to the decline of rural America.

[18]Robinson to Smith, Oct. 15, 1896, Untriangulated Stars, p. 260.

[19]Of general books dealing with American thought in post-Civil War America the following have influenced my interpretations. Paul F. Boller, American Thought in Transition (Chicago, 1971); Oscar Cargill, Intellectual America (New York, 1959); Commager, op. cit.; Merle Curti, The Growth of American Thought (New York, 1964); Ralph H. Gabriel, The Course of American Democratic Thought (New York, 1940); Ronald Lora, Conservative Minds in America (Chicago, 1971); Lloyd Morris, Postscript to Yesterday, American Life and Thought 1876-1946 (New York, 1947); Roderick Nash, The Nervous Generation: American Thought 1917-1930 (Chicago, 1970); Harvey Wish, Society and Thought in Modern America (New York, 1952).

[20]Hagedorn's account of Harvard and the years after, op. cit., pp. 62-95, is best read in combination with Smith, op. cit., pp. 112-28.

[21]Estelle Kaplan, Philosophy in the Poetry of Edwin Arlington Robinson (New York, 1940) is a good analysis tending to overstate its claims.

[22]W.R. Robinson, "E.A. Robinson's Yankee Conscience," Appreciation of Edwin Arlington Robinson, pp. 322-334 successfully elaborates this aspect of Robinson's personality.

[23]Robinson to Daniel Gregory Mason, Aug. 267, 1899, Selected Letters, p. 20.

[24]Franchere, op. cit., p. 23.

[25]Robinson to Smith, Nov. 6, 1896, Untriangulated Stars, p. 263.

[26]Quoted in Franchere, op. cit., p. 37.

[27]Collected Poems, p. 83.

[28]Ibid, p. 92.

[29]Ibid, p. 85.

NOTES
CHAPTER II

1Quoted in Hagedorn, op. cit., p. 156.

2For the history of the city see Constance McLoughlin
Green, The Rise of Urban America (New York, 1965), a
general account; Blake McKelvey, The Urbanization of
America: 1860-1915 (New Brunswick, N.J., 1963) is more
concentrated, corresponding to Robinson's time; Morton
White and Lucia White, The Intellectual and the City:
From Thomas Jefferson to Frank Lloyd Wright (Cambridge,
Mass., 1962) and Robert H. Walker, The Poet and the
Gilded Age (New York, 1969) should also be consulted.

3Collected Poems, p. 83.

4For New York City in addition to Jacob Riis, How the
Other Half Lives (New York, 1957) see Thomas C.
Cochran, et al, The Greater City: New York 1898-1948
(New York, 1949) and August Cerillo, Jr., "The Impact of
Reform Ideology [in New York City]" in The Age of Urban
Reform, M.H. Ebner and E.M. Tobin, Editors (Port
Washington, 1977), pp. 68-85.

5For a full and interesting treatment of Cohen by his
daughter consult Leonora Rosenfield, Portrait of a
Philosopher (New York, 1962).

6Louis Coxe, Edwin Arlington Robinson The Life of
Poetry, (New York, 1969) has pointed references to
Robinson and alcohol.

7Robinson to Daniel Gregory Mason, Oct. 30, 1899,
Selected Letters, p. 25.

8Robinson to Daniel Gregory Mason, Aug. 27, 1899, Ibid,
p. 20.

9Robinson to Smith, June 3, 1894, Untriangulated Stars,

p. 160.

[10]"Captain Craig," Collected Poems, pp. 113-169.

[11]Ibid, p. 113.

[12]Ibid, p. 117.

[13]Ibid, p. 166.

[14]Ibid, p. 117.

[15]Hagedorn, op. cit., pp. 156-174; pp. 193-223 best tells the story of Robinson down and out in New York and of his friendship with Roosevelt.

[16]For a specialized statement on this aspect of Roosevelt see David H. Burton, "The President as Literary Critic," Four Quarters, Vol. XXIII, No. 3, Spring, 1974, pp. 17-25.

[17]Robinson to Craven Lonstroth Betts, April 28, 1905, Selected Letters, p. 60.

[18]Hagedorn, op. cit., p. 216.

[19]Roosevelt, The Works of Theodore Roosevelt, 24 volumes, Literary Essays, volume 14 (New York, 1924), pp. 360-364; 360.

[20]For an examination of the mind of Roosevelt see Edward J. Wagenknecht, The Seven Worlds of Theodore Roosevelt (New York, 1958); David H. Burton's Theodore Roosevelt, (New York, 1972) is an intellectual biography.

[21]Robinson to Daniel Gregory Mason, June 19, 1899, Selected Letters, p. 17.

[22]Robinson to Smith, May 17, 1897, <u>Untriangulated</u> <u>Stars</u>, p. 286.

[23]<u>Collected</u> <u>Poems</u>, pp. 317-19.

[24]"John Brown," <u>Ibid</u>, pp. 485-490.

[25]<u>Ibid</u>, pp. 474-484.

[26]<u>Ibid</u>, pp. 359-361.

[27]<u>Ibid</u>, p. 360.

[28]<u>Ibid</u>, p. 340.

[29]<u>Ibid</u>, pp. 350-353.

[30]<u>Ibid</u>, pp. 330-331.

[31]<u>Ibid</u>, pp. 319-323.

[32]<u>Ibid</u>, pp. 347-348.

[33]Hagedorn has a charming and authoritative account. <u>op.</u> <u>cit.</u>, pp. 261-271.

[34]<u>Ibid</u>, p. 271.

[35]<u>Collected</u> <u>Poems</u>, pp. 60-71.

[36]<u>Ibid</u>, p. 65.

[37]Robinson to Hermann Hagedorn, Dec. 15, 1913, <u>Selected</u> <u>Letters</u>, pp. 80-81.

[38]Collected Poems, p. 64.

[39]Hagedorn, op. cit., p. 302.

[40]Robinson to Louis Ledoux, March 18, 1916, Selected Letters, p. 92.

[41]Robinson to Lowell, March 18, 1916, ibid, p. 93.

[42]Robinson to Gardiner, Nov. 2, 1898, ibid, pp. 15-6.

[43]Robinson to Durant, Sept. 18, 1931, ibid, pp. 163-164.

NOTES
CHAPTER III

[1] Books which examine the era of war, peace, prosperity and depression include Preston Slosson, The Great Crusade and After, 1914-1928 (New York, 1931), Frederick Paxson, American Democracy and the World War (New York, 1931), Frederick Paxson, American Democracy and the World War, 3 volumes (Boston, 1936-1948); Josephus Daniels, The Wilson Era: Years of War and After, 1917-1923 (Chapel Hill, 1946), William E. Leuchtenburg, The Perils of Prosperity, 1914-1932 (Chicago, 1958), and John D. Hicks, The Republican Ascendency, 1921-1933 (New York, 1960).

[2] Collected Poems, pp. 11-12.

[3] Hagedorn, op. cit., pp. 302-3.

[4] Collected Poems, p. 11.

[5] Ibid, p. 12.

[6] Ibid.

[7] "John Dewey, "The Need for a Recovery of Philosophy," in Creative Intelligence (New York, 1917), pp. 8-68; especially pp. 55ff.

[8] Randolph Bourne, War and the Intellectuals (New York, 1964).

[9] John C. Farrell, Beloved Lady: A History of Jane Addams' Ideas on Reform and Peace (Baltimore, 1967), pp. 140ff.

[10] "Editorial," The Catholic World, CV, 626, May 1917, p. 152.

[11]Robinson to Edith Brower, June 2, 1918, Edwin
Arlington Robinson's Letters to Edith Brower, Richard
Cary, Editor (Cambridge, Mass., 1968), p. 172.
(Hereafter cited as Brower Letters).

[12]Robinson to Mrs. Louis V. Ledoux, July 30, 1916,
Selected Letters, p. 97.

[13]Collected Poems, pp. 235-314.

[14]Ibid, p. 289.

[15]Ibid, p. 251.

[16]Ibid, p. 258.

[17]Ibid, p. 251.

[18]Ibid, p. 289.

[19]Ibid, p. 290.

[20]Ibid.

[21]Robinson to Hagedorn, Sept. 8, 1918, Selected Letters,
p. 113.

[22]Collected Poems, p. 242.

[23]Ibid, p. 297.

[24]Ibid, pp. 365-449.

[25]Robinson to Hagedorn, September 8, 1918, Selected
Letters, p. 113.

[26]Collected Poems, p. 419; p. 421.

[27]Ibid, p. 403.

[28]Robinson to Hagedorn, Sept. 8, 1913, Selected Letters, p. 113. On the meaning of Lancelot Robinson wrote that "if one insists, Lancelot, in this poem, and in L&G., may be taken as a rather distant symbol of Germany, though the reader will do well not to make too much of this or to carry it too far." Ibid, p. 112.

[29]Robinson wrote a cryptic note to Hagedorn in October, 1918. "I was a little hasty about our ground listening President, but I don't yet feel sure he won't spill the beans." Robinson to Hagedorn, Oct. 17, 1918, Selected Letters, pp. 113-4.

[30] Robinson to Mabel Dodge Sterne, March 12, 1919, ibid, p. 115. That Robinson continued to think about public matters is illustrated in a letter to Edith Brower in which he wrote: "... I have to bristle and spit at any League of Nations that would include this mishandled republic of ours. We would get into all sorts of a mess if anything really happened. So I believe in a League of Europe and let it go at that -- though I don't see how such a thing can be with Russia and Mussolini in the way. Sooner or later the yellow men will come over and get us, and in about five thousand years there may not be any white folks left." Robinson to Brower, Nov. 10, 1929, Brower Letters, p. 198.

[31]Collected Poems, p. 902.

[32]Robinson to Sterne, March 12, 1919, Selected Letters, p. 115.

[33]Robinson to Percy Mackaye, Sept., 29, 1920, ibid, p. 121.

[34] Ibid.

[35] Lively accounts of a lively era are to be found in Frederick L. Allen, Only Yesterday (New York, 1931), and Karl Schriftgiesser, This Was Normalcy (Boston, 1948).

[36] For assessments of the state of religion see H. Paul Douglas, "Protestant Faiths," pp. 505-527 and Francis X. Talbot, "Catholicism in America," pp. 528-542, in America Now, Harold E. Sterns, Editor (New York, 1938).

[37] Bruce Barton, The Man Nobody Knows (New York, 1925).

[38] Robinson to Laura E. Richards, July 31, 1924, Selected Letters, p. 137.

[39] Robinson to Writter Bynner, Oct. 14, 1921, ibid, p. 128.

[40] Collected Poems, pp. 578-9.

[41] Ibid, pp. 471-2.

[42] Ibid, pp. 859-870.

[43] Ibid, p. 861.

[44] Ibid.

[45] Ibid, p. 862.

[46] Ibid, pp. 904-18.

[47] Ibid, p. 909.

[48] Ibid.

[49] Ibid.

[50] Ibid, p. 917. Robinson was outspoken in his correspondence. "The timidity of our public men, who might really do something if they had the courage and vision of as many cockroaches, fills me with dismay and disgust. And their unanimity in forgetting the Fifteenth Amendment while they bury their heads in the sand before the Eighteenth, doesn't make them [any] the more impressive." Robinson to Brower, Sept. 24, 1925, Brower Letters, pp. 186-7. "Oh, no, I don't want the world drunk," he wrote. "On the other hand, I don't want a world tyrannized by Henry Fords, W.J. Bryands, and Charles Bryans W. Eliots -- which appears to be on the way." Robinson to Laura E. Richards, Sept. 21, 1924, Selected Letters, p. 140.

[51] Frederick J. Hoffman, Twenties: American Writing in the Postwar Decade (New York, 1965) gives the broad background.

[52] Irving Babbitt, Democracy and Leadership (Boston, 1924). Babbitt is critically examined in Lora, op. cit., pp. 69-83.

[53] John Dewey, Individualism: Old and New (New York, 1930), pp. 121ff.

[54] Mary Austin, "Artist Life in the United States," The Nation, CXX, No. 3110, Feb. 11, 1925, pp. 151-152; Theodore Dreiser, "America and the Artist," ibid, No. 3119, April 15, 1925, pp. 423-25; Sherwood Anderson, "Living in America," ibid, No. 3127, June 10, 1925, pp. 657-658.

[55] Collected Poems, pp. 460-61.

[56] Ibid, pp. 1179-1187.

[57] Ibid, p. 1183.

[58] Ibid.

[59] Ibid, p. 1181.

[60] Robinson to Smith, Dec. 7, 1896, Untriangulated Stars, pp. 265-66.

[61] Robinson to Daniel Gregory Mason, April 18, 1900, Selected Letters, p. 29.

[62] Robinson to Smith, March 10, 1891, Untriangulated Stars, p. 14.

[63] Collected Poems, pp. 595-720.

[64] Ibid, p. 618.

[65] Robinson took up the problem of the love potion in his letters. "The fool potion, or philtre in the Tristram story has always been an incurable source of annoyance to me, and after fighting it away for four or five years I have finally succumbed to telling the story of what might have happened to human beings in those circumstances, without their wits and will having been taken away by some impossible and wholly superfluous concoction." Robinson to Laura E. Richards, July 26, 1925, Selected Letters, p. 145. See also Robinson to Edith Brower, September 24, 1925, Brower Letters, p. 186.

[66] Collected Poems, pp. 1397-1488.

[67] Ibid, p. 1471.

[68] Ibid, p. 1460.

[69]*Ibid*, p. 1402.

[70]"For a few hours I fancied that our so-called
civilization might not be going after all -- though of
course it is. The whole western world is going to be
blown to pieces, asphyxiated, and starved, and then, for
a few centuries we poor artists are going to have a hard
time. There may not be any, in fact, for they will have
either to die or to dig; and if they dig they can't
compose any Tristrams,or paint any pictures, or write
any poetry. If they did, no one would pay any
attention, for all the rest of the world would be too
much occupied with staying alive." Robinson to Mrs.
Louis V. Ledoux, Feb. 1921, *Selected* *Letters*, pp. 124-
125.

[1]Frederick J. Hoffman, Freudianism and the Literary Mind (New York, 1945) is a good introduction. Lionel Trilling, "Freud and Literature," The Liberal Imagination (New York, 1953), pp. 32-54 is standard.

[2]Alfred Kreymborg, Our Singing Strength (New York, 1929), p. 298.

[3]Theodore Maynard, Our Best Poets (New York, 1922), p. 161. Paul H. Morrill writes of the psychological aspects of Robinson's poetry in "The World Is ... A Kind of Spiritual Kindergarten," Appreciation of Edwin Arlington Robinson, pp. 346-356.

4T.K. Whipple, Spokesmen (New York, 1924), p. 57.

[5]Russell Blakenship, American Literature (New York, 1949), p. 585.

[6]Whipple, op. cit., p. 48.

7Collected Poems, p. 346.

[8]Ibid, pp. 543-573.

[9]John Farrar, "E.A. Robinson's Dime Novel," The Bookman, vol. 53, no. 3, May, 1921, p. 248.

[10]Collected Poems, p. 548.

[11]Ibid, p. 559.

[12]Ibid, p. 554.

[13]Ibid, p. 567.

[14]Ibid, p. 573.

[15]Ibid, pp. 921-957.

[16]Ibid, p. 935.

[17]Ibid, p. 933.

[18]Ibid, p. 923.

[19]Kaplan, op. cit., p. 70.

[20]Collected Poems, p. 956.

[21]Ibid, pp. 961-1007.

[22]Lawrence Friedman, A History of American Law (New York, 1973) is a readable, authoritative study.

[23] Jerome N. Frank, Law and the Modern Mind (New York, 1930) should be supplemented with J. Mitchell Rosenberg, Jerome Frank: Jurist and Philosopher (New York, 1970).

[24] Frank, op. cit., p.

[25] Collected Poems, p. 972.

[26] Ibid, p. 982.

[27] Ibid, p. 963.

[28] Cargill, op. cit., treats these writers in some detail but Robinson appears only occasionally in his account. Robinson had some doubts about long poems: "A long poem nowadays is at best a getting down on one's knees to invite disaster, and with everything going so fast in no apparent direction, it is quite possible that even short poems in the future will have about all they can do to survive." To Edith Brower, Sept. 24, 1925, Brower Letters, p. 186. See also Robinson to Mabel Dodge Luhan, Nov. 15, 1933, Selected Letters, p. 173.

[29] Collected Poems, pp. 1011-1073.

[30] American philanthropy is discussed in Joseph C. Goulden, The Money Givers (New York, 1971) and Merrimom Cuninggim, Private Money and Public Service (New York, 1972).

[31] Collected Poems, p. 1016.

[32] Ibid, p. 1048.

[33] Ibid, p. 1054.

[34] Ibid, p. 1036.

[35] Ibid, pp. 1077-1155.

[36] Ibid, p. 1106.

[37] Ibid, p. 1116.

[38] Ibid, p. 1129.

[39] Ibid, p. 1151.

[40] Ibid, pp. 1231-1307.

[41] Ibid, pp. 1311-1393.

[42] Ibid, p. 1337.

[43] Harold P. Stearns, "The Intellectual Life," Civilization in the United States (New York, 1922), pp. 135-150.

[44]Joseph Wood Krutch, "Modern Temper," The Atlantic Monthly, CXXXIX, Feb. 1927, pp. 166-175.

[45]Carl L. Becker, The Heavenly City of the Eighteenth Century Philosophers (New Haven, 1932), especially pp. 11-18.

[46]Commager, op. cit., p. 160.

47Carl L. Becker, New Liberties For Old (New Haven, 1941), especially pp. 144-151.

NOTES
CHAPTER V

1See Morill, loc. cit., pp. 346-7.

2Robinson to Arthur R. Gledhill, Oct. 28, 1896, Selected Letters, p. 13.

3Collected Poems, p. 903.

4Robinson to Laura E. Richards, Jan. 20, 1933, Selected Letters, p. 169.

5Robinson to Laura E. Richards, Feb. 13, 1933, ibid, p. 170.

6Winthrop S. Hudson, American Protestantism (Chicago, 1961), pp. 120-153.

7William T. Walsh "Some Recollections of E.A. Robinson" Part II, The Catholic World, CLV, (Sept. 1942), pp. 703-712.

8Maynard, The World I Saw (Milwaukee, 1938), p. 238.

9Collected Poems, pp. 1187-1199.

10Walsh, loc. cit., p. 710.

11Collected Poems, pp. 1198-9.

12Ibid, pp. 1159-1169.

13Ibid, p. 1162.

[14]Ibid, p. 1164.

[15]Ibid, p. 1168.

[16]Ibid.

[17]Edwin S. Fussell, "The English Bible," in Edwin Arlington Robinson The Literary Background of a Traditional Poet (Berkeley, 1954), pp. 155-170 shows the influence of the Bible. See also Nicholas Ayo, "Robinson's Use of the Bible," Appreciation of Edwin Arlington Robinson, pp. 262-275.

[18]Robinson to Laura E. Richards, Sept. 11, 1934, Selected Letters, p. 177. But this should be contrasted with a letter to the same correspondent written only a few years before: "If there shouldn't happen to be any next world or any that we remember ... we shall go on somehow or other. I get no comfort out of turning into grass, and cannot believe that the great Whatever-it-is would have gone to so much trouble as to make you and me (not to mention a few others) for the sake of a little ultimate hay." Robinson to Richards, Jan. 19, 1925, ibid, p. 142.

[19]Collected Poems, p. 41.

[20]"Thalia," quoted in Charles Beecher Hogan's A Bibliography of Edwin Arlington Robinson (New Haven, 1936), p. 167.

[21]Robinson, The Children of the Night (Boston, 1897), p. 12.

[22]Ibid.

[23]Ibid.

[24]Amy Lowell, Poetry and Poets (Boston, 1930), p. 26.

[25]*Collected Poems*, pp. 60-69.

[26]*Ibid*, p. 60.

[27]*Ibid*, p. 68.

[28]*Ibid*, p. 67.

[29]*Ibid*, pp. 113-169.

[30]*Ibid*, pp. 1212.

[31]*Ibid*, p. 119.

[32]*Ibid*, p. 151.

[33]*Ibid*, p. 94.

[34]*Ibid*, p. 83.

[35]*Ibid*, pp. 733-856.

[36]*Ibid*, p. 733.

[37]*Ibid*.

BIBLIOGRAPHY
Poems and Letters

Collected Poems of Edwin Arlington Robinson (New York, 1948).

Selected Letters of Edwin Arlington Robinson, Ridgely Torrence, editor (New York, 1940).

Untriangulated Stars: Letters of Edwin Arlington Robinson to Harry deForest Smith, 1890-1905, Denham Sutcliffe, editor (Cambridge, Mass., 1947).

Edwin Arlington Robinson's Letters to Edith Brower, Richard Cary, editor (Cambridge, Mass., 1968).

Biography/Criticism

Barnard, Ellsworth, Edwin Arlington Robinson (New York, 1952).

Brown, Rollo, Next Door To A Poet (New York, 1937).

Cary, Richard, editor, Appreciation of Edwin Arlington Robinson (Waterville, Maine, 1969).

Cestre, Charles, Edwin Arlington Robinson (New York, 1930).

Coxe, Louis, Edwin Arlington Robinson (New York, 1969).

Franchere, Hoyt C., Edwin Arlington Robinson (New York, 1968).

Fussell, Edwin S., Edwin Arlington Robinson: The Literary Background of a Traditional Poet (Berkeley, 1954).

Hagedorn, Hermann, Edwin Arlington Robinson (New York, 1939).

Kaplan, Estelle, Philosophy in the Poetry of Edwin Arlington Robinson (New York, 1940).

Neff, Emery, Edwin Arlington Robinson (New York, 1948).

Robinson, W.R., Edwin Arlington Robinson: A Poetry of the Act (Cleveland, O., 1967).

Smith, Chard Powers, Where the Light Falls: A Portrait of Edwin Arlington Robinson (New York, 1965).

Winters, Yvor, Edwin Arlington Robinson (Norwalk, Conn., 1946).

BIBLIOGRAPHY
Selected General Works

Allen, Frederick L., Only Yesterday (New York, 1931).

Babbitt, Irving, Democracy and Leadership (Boston, 1924).

Beard, Charles A. and Mary R., The Rise of American Civilization (New York, 1930).

Becker, Carl L., The Heavenly City of the Eighteenth Century Philosophers (New Haven, 1932). New Liberties For Old, (New York, 1941).

Blakenship, Russell, American Literature (New York, 1949).

Boller, Paul F., American Thought in Transition (Chicago, 1971).

Bourne, Randolph, War and the Intellectuals (New York, 1964).

Brooks, Van Wyck, New England: Indian Summer (New York, 1940).

Cargill, Oscar, Intellectual America (New York, 1959).

Commager, Henry Steele, The American Mind (New Haven, 1950).

Curti, Merle, The Growth of American Thought (New York, 1964).

Friedman, Lawrence, A History of American Law (New York, 1973).

Gabriel, Ralph H., The Course of American Democratic Thought (New York, 1940).

Goulden, Joseph C., The Money Givers (New York, 1971).

Hoffman, Frederick J., Freudianism and the Literary Mind (New York, 1945). Twenties: American Writing in the Postwar Decade, (New York, 1945).

Hudson, Winthrop, American Protestantism (Chicago, 1961).

Krutch, Joseph Wood, The Modern Temper (New York, 1929).

Kouwenhoven, John A., Made in America The Arts in Modern Civilization (New York, 1948).

Leuchtenburg, William E., The Perils of Prosperity, 1914-1932 (Chicago, 1958).

Lora, Ronald, Conservative Minds in America (Chicago, 1971).

May, Henry F., The End of American Innocence (Chicago, 1964).

McKelvey, Blake, The Urbanization of America: 1860-1915 (New Brunswick, N.J.).

Morris, Lloyd, Postscript to Yesterday American Life and Thought 1896-1946, (New York, 1947).

Nash, Roderick, The Nervous Generation: American Thought, 1917-1930 (Chicago, 1971).

Paxson, Frederick, American Democracy and the World War, 3 volumes (Boston, 1936-1948).

Schriftgeisser, Karl, This Was Normalcy (Boston, 1948).

Slosson, Preston, The Great Crusade and After, 1914-1928 (New York, 1931).

Stearns, Harold E., America Now (New York, 1938).

Trilling, Lionel, The Liberal Imagination (New York, 1953).

Wagenknecht, Edward J., The Seven Worlds of Theodore Roosevelt (New York, 1958).

Walker, Robert H., The Poet and the Gilded Age (New York, 1969).

Wish, Harvey, Society and Thought in Modern America (New York, 1952).

White, Morton and Lucia, The Intellectual and the City: From Thomas Jefferson to Frank Lloyd Wright (Cambridge, Mass., 1962).

INDEX